✓ *How to Pass*

NATIONAL 5

Mod
Stud

Frank Cooney, Paul
Gary Hughes and D

**HODDER
GIBSON**
AN HACHETTE UK COMPANY

The Publishers would like to thank the following for permission to reproduce copyright material:

Photo credits

p.12 © ERIC PIERMONT/AFP/Getty Images; **p.16** (left to right) © The Scottish National Party, © The Scottish Labour Party, © The Scottish Conservative Party, © The Scottish Liberal Democrats Party; **p.24** © Ramil Sitdikov/Host Photo Agency via Getty Images; **p.28** (left to right) © The Conservative Party, © The Labour Party, © The Liberal Democrats Party; **p.39** © Ken McKay/ITV via Getty Images; **p.50** © Malcolm Fife / Alamy; **p.54** © Stockbyte/Getty Images / Design Essentials EO005; **p.60** © Monkey Business - Fotolia.com; **p.62** © REX/Henry Langston; **p.74** © REX; **p.86** (top to bottom) © STRINGER/AFP/GettyImages, © The African National Congress Party, © The Democratic Alliance Party, © The Inkatha Freedom Party, © The Congress of the People Party; **p.95** © Lintao Zhang/Getty Images; **p.107** © Mike Goldwater / Alamy; **p.111** © Oxfam; **p.117** © REX/Sipa USA; **p.119** (top) © Image Asset Management Ltd. / Alamy, (bottom) © United Nations; **p.120** © incamerastock / Alamy; **p.131** © Solo Syndication.

Acknowledgements

Text extract entitled 'Children's Hearings' on pp. 67–68, content courtesy of SCRA.

Text extract on pp. 129–130 is reproduced courtesy of Metro.

Every effort has been made to trace all copyright holders, but if any have been inadvertently overlooked the Publishers will be pleased to make the necessary arrangements at the first opportunity.

Although every effort has been made to ensure that website addresses are correct at time of going to press, Hodder Gibson cannot be held responsible for the content of any website mentioned in this book. It is sometimes possible to find a relocated web page by typing in the address of the home page for a website in the URL window of your browser.

Hachette UK's policy is to use papers that are natural, renewable and recyclable products and made from wood grown in sustainable forests. The logging and manufacturing processes are expected to conform to the environmental regulations of the country of origin.

Orders: please contact Bookpoint Ltd, 130 Park Drive, Abingdon, Oxon OX14 4SE. Telephone: (44) 01235 827720. Fax: (44) 01235 400454. Lines are open 9.00–5.00, Monday to Saturday, with a 24-hour message answering service. Visit our website at www.hoddereducation.co.uk. Hodder Gibson can be contacted direct on: Tel: 0141 848 1609; Fax: 0141 889 6315; email: hoddergibson@hodder.co.uk

First published in 2014 by
Hodder Gibson, an imprint of Hodder Education,
An Hachette UK Company
2a Christie Street
Paisley PA1 1NB
Impression number   5 4 3 2

Year   2018 2017 2016 2015 2014

Cover photo © Mircea Maties – Fotolia
Illustrations by Aptara, Inc.
Typeset in 13/15 Cronos Pro (Light) by Aptara, Inc.
Printed in India
A catalogue record for this title is available from the British Library
ISBN: 978 1 4441 8735 9

Contents

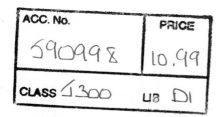

Introduction

This revision book will help you to achieve the best possible result in your Modern Studies National 5 examination by explaining clearly what you need to know about the exam and what knowledge and skills you will need to display.

Access to the Hodder Gibson *National 4 & 5 Modern Studies* textbooks will enhance the use of this revision guide. Each of these books (and this *How to Pass*) has been endorsed by the Scottish Qualifications Authority.

The textbooks are:
- Democracy in Scotland and the UK
- Social Issues in the UK
- World Powers and International Issues.

You have already covered all or most of the skills and knowledge required to pass National 5 but revision has a very important role to play. By working your way through this book you will find it much easier to understand what you need to display in your assessment answers. This will enhance your confidence and enable you to achieve your full potential.

You will also find advice about the assignment, in which you will have to research a Modern Studies topic or issue of your own choice. This assignment is important as it will be marked by SQA and will contribute to your overall mark and grade.

We hope you will find this book of great value and support.

Good luck!

Part One: How you will be tested

The National 5 award is made up of both internally and externally marked assessments. To achieve the award, you need to pass the internal assessment for each of the following units:

- Democracy in Scotland and the United Kingdom
- Social Issues in the United Kingdom
- International Issues.

You also need to pass the Added Value unit for National 5. This is an externally marked assessment that consists of two parts:

- National 5 question paper (60 marks – 75% of your overall mark)
- National 5 assignment (20 marks – 25% of your overall mark).

Total marks available: 80 marks

The marks you achieve in the question paper and assignment are added together and an overall mark will indicate a pass or fail. From this, your course award will then be graded.

Chapter 1

The question paper

The question paper is worth a total of 60 marks, with up to 20 marks awarded for each of the three units. Across the whole exam paper, there are 26 marks for skills-based questions and 34 for knowledge-based questions. Each source-based question will be marked out of eight or ten marks, and each knowledge and understanding question will be marked out of four, six or eight marks. You will have one hour and 30 minutes to complete the question paper.

What types of questions will I need to answer?

There are three types of skills questions that you will have practised in class and answered as part of your unit assessments. These are:

1   Using sources of information to **identify and explain selective use of facts**. This will have been assessed in your Democracy in Scotland and the UK unit.
2   Using sources of information to **make and justify a decision**. This will have been assessed in your Social Issues in the UK unit.
3   Using sources of information to **draw and support conclusions**. This will have been assessed in your International Issues unit.

In Part Three of this book we will look at examples of skills-based questions and students' answers.

Remember

In your course exam, the skills-based questions can appear in any of the three units — so *selective use of facts* could be a question in the International Issues section of the exam.

In the knowledge section of your exam you will answer two types of questions:

1   **Describe** questions, for example:
    Describe, in detail, two ways in which pressure groups try to influence the Scottish government.
2   **Explain** questions, for example:
    Explain, in detail, the advantages and disadvantages of the First Past the Post system (FPTP) that is used to elect the UK parliament.

Remember

In your course exam, the knowledge and skills questions for International Issues will not refer to a particular country or a particular issue. You will be expected to base your answer on your knowledge and understanding of your studied World Power or Issue.

Do I have choice?

Your teacher will usually have chosen one topic from each of the three units for you to study and you will answer questions on these topics in your exam. Your teacher will have chosen from the following options for each unit:

Unit of the course	Option one	Option two
Democracy in Scotland and the UK	Democracy in Scotland	Democracy in the UK
Social Issues in the UK	Social Inequality	Crime and the Law
International Issues	World Powers	World Issues

Hints & tips

What makes a good knowledge answer?

✓ One that answers the question and provides only information that is **relevant** to the question.

✓ One that is **detailed** and written in paragraphs with clear development of the points you wish to discuss. Remember that one very developed *describe* answer can gain three marks and one very developed *explain* answer can gain four marks.

✓ One that is an **appropriate length**. Use the number of marks assigned to each question as a guide to how much you should write. Writing long answers for four-mark questions may make you run out of time in the exam.

✓ One that uses **up-to-date** examples to illustrate your understanding of the question being asked.

What makes a bad knowledge answer?

✓ One that does not answer the question, or tries to change the question being asked. This is sometimes called 'turning a question'.

✓ One that gives detailed description or explanation that is not relevant to the question.

✓ One that contains information that is out of date (you should be especially careful of this in the International Issues unit).

✓ One that simply consists of a list of facts with no development. This can receive a maximum of only two marks. You must tailor your answer to the question, and only give information that is relevant to what is being asked.

Chapter 2
The Assignment

Before your exam in May, you will carry out the 'assignment' as part of your National 5 course assessment. Your teacher will probably plan to complete this during the spring term before you sit the exam.

What is the assignment?

The assignment is your personal research on a Modern Studies topic or issue of your own choice. The information collected should display knowledge and understanding of the topic or issue chosen and should include at least two methods of collecting information, with comment on the effectiveness of the methods used.

You will write up the results of your research under controlled assessment conditions on an official SQA double-page sheet. You will be given one hour to do this.

The assignment is very important as it is worth a total of 20 marks. Of these, fourteen marks are for skills and six marks are for knowledge and understanding.

You are allowed to bring two single-sided sheets of A4 paper (containing your notes) into the exam to refer to during the write-up.

What type of hypothesis or issue should I choose?

With agreement from your teacher, you should choose a topic or issue that you feel is appropriate, for example: *'The voting age in all Scottish and UK elections should be reduced to sixteen'*.

You may choose a **hypothesis** or issue from any of the three course units or you may choose a topic that integrates two units of the course, for example: *'Health inequalities in Scotland and the USA'*.

Some possible titles could include:
- *Voting age should be reduced to sixteen for all UK elections.*
- *Lifestyle choices are the main cause of health inequalities in Scotland.*
- *Poverty was the main cause of the 2011 riots in England.*
- *The 'not proven' verdict does not deliver justice.*
- *The Educational Maintenance Allowance should be given to all 16+ school students.*
- *The abuse of gun ownership is a major problem in the USA but not in Scotland.*
- *The American dream is not a reality for many US citizens.*
- *The war against terror has been won.*

Key words

Hypothesis: A hypothesis is simply a statement that your personal research will try to prove or disprove. If you are being presented at National 5 and you have decided on your topic/issue, it is good practice to state a hypothesis, which you will revisit in your conclusion. However, you could still receive credit for just stating your aims.

Where do I gather information from?

The information gathered for your research can be broken down into two parts: **primary information** and **secondary information**.

Primary information

Primary information is evidence that you have gathered by yourself and is unique to your personal research. If possible, your personal research should contain at least **two** pieces of information gathered by primary research, as well as information gathered from other sources. The ways in which you gather primary evidence can vary greatly – some examples are below:

- surveys/questionnaires
- interviews
- emails
- letters
- focus groups
- field study.

Secondary information

Secondary information is evidence that you have gathered from research that was carried out by others. You should use it to help support your personal research. There is a vast amount of secondary information available, in many different formats – below are just a few examples:

- school textbooks, newspapers and magazines
- internet search engines and websites
- TV and radio programmes
- mobile phone apps
- social media such as Twitter
- library books and articles.

You are expected to evaluate the strengths and weaknesses of each research method you use and to analyse your findings. Remember that two methods is the minimum you are required to use and you might wish to widen your range to more than two.

Remember

For the write-up of your research you will need to refer to only **two** of your research methods. You can include your findings in your notes that you bring in to the exam, as you must refer to these findings in your write-up.

How do I plan my research?

In order to carry out a successful piece of personal research you need to plan it effectively. You will need to keep all evidence of your planning so that your work can be accurately marked.

You may wish to consider the following questions about your primary and secondary sources:

- What useful information have I got from each source to help me research my issue?
- How reliable is the information gathered from each source?
- Could the sources contain bias or exaggeration?

What is a 'pro forma' assignment sheet?

As part of the assignment, you need to demonstrate your understanding, analysis and evaluation of the information you have collected. A self-assessment 'pro forma' sheet can be used to do this. The pro forma sheet consists of four sections for you to fill in, with marks allocated to each. Below is an outline of the sections.

1 Research question (2 marks)

Your topic should be relevant to Modern Studies and you may discuss your choice with your teacher. The best practice is to present the research question in the form of a hypothesis with clear aims. Do not choose a vague and unfocused topic such as '*A study of poverty in Scotland*'; a better title would be '*The 2013 "bedroom tax" is a tax on the disabled*'. This is written in the form of a hypothesis and allows you to consider to what extent the statement is correct and to consider the evidence that supports and disagrees with the hypothesis. You should also consider whether the evidence you research is correct or exaggerated.

2 Research methods: Collecting relevant evidence from at least two sources (8 marks)

You are expected to evaluate the strengths and weaknesses of the two research methods you have used. You should explain why each method is relevant and highlight its strengths and/or weaknesses. You should make reference to the information that you will take into the assignment.

3 Research findings: Presenting your findings clearly (6 marks)

You will have a full page to detail and explain the evidence you have gathered. You may wish to write more and may request extra sheets. The evidence should be balanced and factually correct and you should consider various viewpoints. You should make reference to your A4 information sheet (the notes you bring into the assignment write-up) in your presentation of your findings. Your A4 information sheet should include evidence of primary and/or secondary research and may include, for example, survey results, interview findings, notes from a textbook, newspapers or websites.

4 Research conclusion (4 marks)

Your conclusion should be based on the quality of the research evidence you have presented and should link back to your original hypothesis. Try to avoid just repeating findings already given. At this stage you can indicate what your final thoughts on your issue are.

Remember

Try to base your assignment around a hypothesis rather than just a general study of an issue.

Part Two: Democracy in Scotland and the UK

This section of the book provides summary course notes for the Democracy in Scotland and the UK unit of the course.

In the knowledge section of the exam you will answer **one describe question** and **one explain question** on this unit and these questions will be marked out of four, six or eight marks each.

What you should know

To be successful in this section, you should:

★ be able to **explain** the relationships between each part of the UK political system, including the Scottish parliament and the UK parliament
★ be **aware** of some of the main issues in the UK political system, including the referendum on Scottish independence.

Introduction to democracy

In a democracy, citizens can participate freely through voting to elect their political representatives. They also have the right to free speech, to join pressure groups and trade unions, and to criticise the government.

Rights and responsibilities

A right is something a person is entitled to; responsibilities are things that people should do or are expected to do. Table 3.1 summarises our rights and responsibilities as citizens of the United Kingdom.

Rights	Responsibilities
To elect our representatives and vote on political issues.	To accept the decision of the majority, even if we disagree.
Those eighteen years old and over can vote in elections.	To be responsible citizens and use our vote in an attempt to influence our representatives.
To express our views in print, on social network sites and in newspapers.	To avoid telling lies or slandering individuals, since this is illegal.
To protest and try to change government legislation such as student tuition fees.	To protest within the law and respect the rights of others.

Table 3.1 Rights and responsibilities

The UK political system

The UK is a parliamentary democracy with a constitutional monarch. This means that the Queen is the ceremonial head of state to the peoples of England, Scotland, Northern Ireland and Wales, but not the head of government.

Figure 3.1 illustrates Scotland's place in the UK political system. The traditional **prerogative powers** of the monarch are held by the UK prime minister and the cabinet. The UK is a unitary system where all powers are vested in the UK parliament. In this way, the monarch's role in the UK is mostly ceremonial. The UK government is directly accountable to parliament.

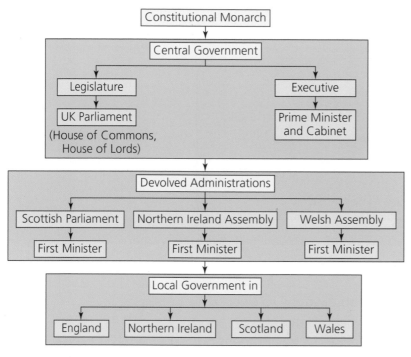

Figure 3.1 The structure of the UK political system

How are decisions made in the UK?

There are two types of democracy: **direct democracy** and representative democracy. The UK has a total population of 60 million, of which Scotland has around 5.2 million. Direct democracy would be impractical here because of the number of citizens. Instead, the UK is a representative democracy. However, the government can, on occasion, ask the people to vote on a particular issue. This is called a **referendum**. In 2014, the people of Scotland will be able to take part in a referendum on Scottish independence.

Representative democracy

The UK is a representative democracy. This means that UK citizens can vote in elections for the people they want to represent their views. These representatives then take decisions on behalf of the people. If voters do not like the decisions their representatives make on their behalf, they can vote for a different representative, called a candidate, at the next election.

Who makes decisions for us?

MP (member of parliament)	MSP (member of Scottish parliament)
MEP (member of the European parliament)	Local councillor

	Local council elections	Scottish parliament elections	UK parliament elections	European parliament elections
Frequency of elections	Every four years	Every four years	(At least) every five years	Every five years
Number of representatives	1200 local councillors	129 MSPs	650 MPs	6 MEPs (out of 736)
Responsibilities of representatives	Local services, such as education, housing, roads and refuse collection	Devolved powers, such as health, social work, planning, the environment (see table below)	Reserved powers, such as the economy, taxation, foreign affairs, defence (see table below)	Economic and social affairs, such as setting fishing quotas

Table 3.2 Who makes decisions for us?

Devolved powers	Reserved powers
Health	Defence
Education and training	Social security
Social work	Foreign affairs
Housing	Constitutional matters
Local government	Immigration
Tourism and economic development	Broadcasting
Law and home affairs	Trade and industry
Agriculture, forestry and fishing	Energy: nuclear, coal and gas
Planning	Employment legislation
Police and fire services	Equal opportunities
The environment	Fiscal and monetary system
Sports and the arts	Gambling and the National Lottery
Scottish road network and harbours	Data protection

Table 3.3 Devolved and reserved powers

Devolution

The Scottish parliament was established in1999 after the people of Scotland voted in favour of **devolution** in a referendum.

In September 2014, the SNP majority government will hold another referendum to ask the Scottish people the following question:

Should Scotland be an independent country? Yes / No

Whilst the SNP and the Green party will campaign **FOR** independence, Labour, Conservative and Liberal Democrat will all campaign **AGAINST** independence. Due to a change in the law, sixteen and seventeen year olds will be able to vote in the independence referendum.

Key words

Devolution: The transfer of powers from a central body to regional administrations.

Chapter 3
Democracy in Scotland

What you should know

To be successful in this section, you should:
★ **understand** the role of an MSP, both in their constituencies and in parliament, and also the role of a local councillor
★ **know** about the role of the Scottish parliament, including the functions of the chamber and committees. You must also have sound knowledge of the work of local councils
★ have a good **knowledge** about participation and representation in Scotland:

  ★ have a working **knowledge** of political parties in Scotland and their main policies
  ★ **understand** the purpose of an election campaign and its main features
  ★ **understand** the advantages and disadvantages of the proportional representation systems used in Scotland – the Additional Member System in the Scottish parliament and the Single Transferable Vote in local authority elections.

> **Hints & tips** ⭐
>
> *In your exam you should try to include examples whenever possible. Go to www.theyworkforyou.com and find out who your MSPs are. You can use them as an example of MSPs.*

Representation

Everyone in Scotland has a constituency MSP and seven regional MSPs elected to the Scottish parliament. Scotland is divided into two groups of geographical areas, called constituencies and regions. There are 73 constituencies, each with its own constituency MSP. These constituencies lie within eight regions and each region has seven 'list' MSPs, giving a total of 56 regional MSPs. This gives a total of 129 MSPs within the Scottish parliament.

> **Hints & tips**
>
> *Visit www.scottish. parliament.uk/ msps/9959.aspx to see a map of the eight regions and constituency maps for each region.*

The role of an MSP

An MSP's working life is divided into two distinct roles: work within their constituency/region; and work within the Scottish parliament.

> **Hints & tips**
>
> *An exam question could be based on the work carried out within an MSP's constituency or region, or the work they carry out at parliament.*

Parliamentary work	Constituency work
Debating: Every MSP will participate in some debates. This gives MSPs the chance to put forward the views of their constituents. For example, if there are plans to reduce the number of nurses in the NHS within Scotland, this may directly affect some constituencies with hospitals, e.g. Edinburgh Royal Infirmary.	**Surgeries:** Usually scheduled once a week, an MSP will visit various areas within their constituency or region for an open advice clinic, known as a surgery. Constituents can drop in to the surgery to express concerns that they have directly to their MSP. These concerns could be about local issues as well as national issues.
Voting on new laws: Every MSP has to vote on whether they agree or disagree with each proposed new law, known as a Bill. For example, they could vote for or against a proposal to lower the voting age to sixteen.	**Attending meetings:** MSPs will attend a huge number of meetings when they are in their constituencies. For example, he or she may meet local charities to listen to their views on current government policy.
Question time (FMQT): Every government department will have a 'question time' within parliament where MSPs get the chance to question the government directly. At first minister's question time (FMQT), an MSP could have the chance to challenge the FM directly about government decisions and express his or her constituents' concerns.	**Local media:** In order to keep a good profile within their constituency or region MSPs will often appear in local newspapers or on local TV and radio. Quite often MSPs will raise awareness of local issues or highlight local charities using the media and communicate their thoughts about these.
Committee work: MSPs can become members of a committee. This gives them an opportunity to look at a specific issue in depth. An example of this is that if an MSP is interested in educational issues they could sit on the Education and Culture Committee, perhaps looking at the impact of a Curriculum for Excellence.	**Visits and social events:** An MSP is often regarded as a high profile guest for many different organisations and as a result MSPs will spend a large proportion of their time to attending various events, for example the opening of a new business or a school's awards ceremony.
Written answers: An MSP can submit a written question to the government and receive a reply. He or she could then relay this to a concerned constituent.	**Local party meetings:** MSPs will meet occasionally with local party members to discuss issues that concern the party as a whole. The MSP will then relay this information to the party's leadership.
Members' Bills: MSPs also have the chance to submit their own ideas for new laws. Every year they can submit up to two of their own Bills. If they pass through parliament they could become new laws. Margo MacDonald MSP submitted her own Assisted Suicide Bill; however, this has not been successfully passed through the Scottish parliament.	**Constituent letters, emails and social media:** MSPs receive a large volume of letters and emails from constituents and local groups on local and national issues. In order to manage this, MSPs will have a constituency office and employ a number of staff. Increasingly, MSPs also use social media such Twitter and Facebook to communicate with constituents and hear their views.

Table 3.4 The role of an MSP

The Scottish parliament

All the MSPs elected to the Scottish parliament work within the debating chamber of the parliament. The governing party sits in the middle of the chamber and the opposition parties sit on either side.

Remember

Unlike the UK parliament, the Scottish parliament only has one chamber, called the debating chamber, which is fully elected. The UK parliament has two chambers. The House of Commons is elected; the House of Lords is an appointed chamber.

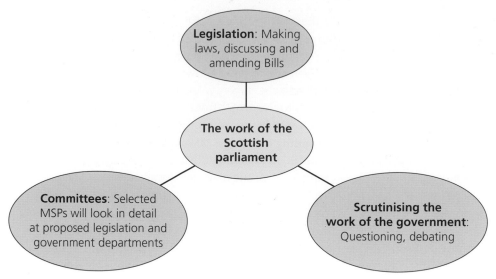

Figure 3.2 The work of the Scottish parliament

Roles within the Scottish parliament

First minister

The first minister is the leader of the governing party. In most cases this will be the party with the most seats in the chamber. Due to the **party whip**, government MSPs usually obey the first minister's wishes. The first minister also has the power to appoint whom he wants to the cabinet and this gives him **power of patronage**. If his party's MSPs have ambitions to gain a position in the cabinet they would do well to fully support their party leader. The first minister is accountable to the Scottish parliament.

Figure 3.3 The current First Minister Alex Salmond

Key words

Party whip: The party whip is appointed by the leadership of a political party to persuade or pressurise MSPs into supporting the party – this is called following the party line.

Power of patronage: The power to appoint or remove individuals from office.

Cabinet

The first minister appoints MSPs from his or her party to run government departments. There is a government department to look after each of the devolved powers listed in Table 3.3. Two of the most powerful positions in the cabinet are the finance secretary, in charge of government finances, and the deputy first minister, who works closely with the first minister in shaping policy.

Leaders of opposition parties

The current leaders of the opposition parties are Johann Lamont (Labour), Ruth Davidson (Conservative) and Willie Rennie (Liberal Democrat). The leaders of the opposition parties are seen as the chief critics of the government, but they do not have any direct power within the chamber. The opposition parties select MSPs from their own parties to form a **shadow cabinet**, which scrutinises the policies and decisions of the government departments.

Public petitions

Members of the public can raise a 'national issue' with parliament by registering a public petition. The Public Petitions Committee will consider what action should be taken. Public petitions have resulted in:

- a ban on smoking in public places
- plans to restore a railway link to the Borders.

How representative is the Scottish parliament?

Ethnic minorities and women have not been well represented in the Scottish parliament since it was established in 1999.

There are currently two MSPs from a non-white background – less than 2% of all MSPs. The Scottish ethnic minority population is around 8%.

Women are also not fairly represented in the Scottish parliament. Only 35% of MSPs are female (44 out of 129 MSPs), though 51% of the Scottish population is female.

Why is female representation in the Scottish parliament higher than the UK parliament?

In the UK parliament, 22% of MPs are female, compared to 35% in the Scottish parliament. The reasons for the difference include:

- the working hours of the Scottish parliament are much more family friendly than those of the UK parliament
- there are modern crèche facilities within the parliament
- through the regional vote, political parties can promote more female MSPs.

Hints & tips

Visit www.scottish. parliament.uk/ gettinginvolved/petitions to check out current petitions or even to start one of your own!

Local authorities in Scotland

Local authorities or councils play a major role in people's everyday lives. For example, it is local councils that run our schools, maintain street lighting and collect our household waste. The country is divided into 32 local authority areas that organise and run local services for everyone in Scotland. Decision making at local authority level is done by elected councillors.

The role of a local councillor

Local councillors have a responsibility to help residents in their local area. Their relationship with the people in the area (who are responsible for voting them into the role) is very important.

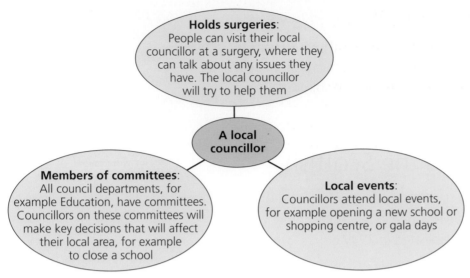

Figure 3.4 The different roles of a local councillor

Local authority departments

Department	Responsibilities
Education and learning	Councils operate local nurseries, primary and secondary schools. They also provide specialist educational provision such as educational psychologists.
Housing	Affordable rented council housing is available across council areas. The council has to maintain and improve their housing stock and provide tenants with benefits advice.
Social work	The social work service aims to protect vulnerable groups within society, with an emphasis on supporting individuals who are at risk. This includes child protection, youth and criminal justice, alcohol and drug services, and care for the elderly.
Roads and transport	Councils look after the local road network and have the responsibility of making sure this network is adequately maintained and safe, including street lighting, traffic signage, traffic calming measures and co-ordinating all road works. The council also manages the gritting and snow-clearing service during the winter.
Environmental services	The council has a responsibility to keep its area clean and tidy. That job involves collecting refuse and recycling, street sweeping, and maintaining parks and open spaces.
Law and licensing	This department deals with various areas, from birth, death and marriage registrations, to licensing and permits for new shops and bars. This department also operates the Sheriff and Justice of Peace courts.
Leisure services	It is important that the council offers a variety of leisure services, such as leisure centres, swimming pools and gyms; it also manages cultural services such as libraries, museums and art galleries.
Planning	The planning department make decisions about future developments and the use of land in the towns, cities and countryside of its area, for example, before the building of a new supermarket, permission must be gained through this department.
Finance	All revenue received by the council through council tax, government grants, housing rent and so on is managed by the finance department. The department also has the responsibility of ensuring the council is operating financially within budget.

Table 3.5 The different local authority departments

What decisions do councillors make?

Councillors have to make decisions that some members of the local community won't agree with. The councillor has to weigh up the wishes of the local community with what he or she believes to be the best course of action. In recent times, decision making has been especially difficult as local authorities have had to cut their budgets drastically. This has meant some council services have had to be reduced or removed altogether.

Scottish council budget cuts

All 32 local councils in Scotland are currently dealing with severe budget cuts. Councils have worked out how much savings are required by 2015. For example:

Argyll and Bute: £18 million savings required

Glasgow City: £127 million savings required

Aberdeenshire: £62 million savings required

North Lanarkshire: £70 million savings required

The biggest expenditure for councils is on staff, so in recent times local authorities have begun to cut a number of positions. For example, East Dunbartonshire plans to cut the number of staff working for the council by 200 posts per year. These job cuts affect employment levels in the local area.

Impact of cuts

There have been a number of cuts made to local services as local authorities attempt to save huge amounts of money by 2015. Glasgow City Council, for example, has changed the frequency of refuse collection from once per week to once per fortnight. In North Lanarkshire, free school buses are no longer available for children who live within three miles of their school.

Political parties in Scotland

There are four main political parties in Scotland: the Scottish National Party, the Scottish Labour Party, the Scottish Conservative Party and the Scottish Liberal Democrat Party. There are also smaller parties such as the Scottish Green Party and the Scottish Socialist Party.

What do political parties do?

Most MSPs and councillors are affiliated with a political party. Once elected, MSPs and councillors connected to a political party are expected to represent the policies of the party.

Before an election, political parties will produce their ideas of how, if elected, they will try to improve the country. These ideas are known as **policies**. As part of the election campaign, the parties will collate these ideas in their **party manifestos**, which voters and the media can read.

The aim of a political party is to win as many seats as possible in an election. The more seats they win, the greater the influence the party will have in how the country is run and the easier it will be for them to put their policies into action.

Key words

Party manifesto: A party publication which contains the policies they hope to implement, if elected.

Political parties in Scotland and their policies

Political party	Scottish National Party	Scottish Labour	Scottish Conservatives	Scottish Liberal Democrats
	SNP www.snp.org	Scottish Labour	Scottish Conservatives	SCOTTISH LIBERAL DEMOCRATS
Leader in 2013	Alex Salmond	Johann Lamont	Ruth Davidson	Willie Rennie
Key policies	● To lead Scotland to independence following the referendum in 2014. ● To maintain free tuition for Scottish students in Scotland.	● Keep Scotland as part of the UK. ● Consider the introduction of tuition fees for Scottish university students.	● Keep Scotland as part of the UK. ● To maintain Scotland's nuclear determent.	● To keep Scotland as part of the United Kingdom but push for more powers for the Scottish parliament. ● To oppose the construction of more nuclear power plants in Scotland.

Table 3.6 Political parties in Scotland and their key policies

The SNP majority Government

Following the 2011 Scottish Parliament elections, the SNP won the election with a majority. This sent shockwaves through Scottish politics, as the Additional Member System (AMS) was designed to prevent any one party gaining an overall majority. Following the victory, the SNP Government has announced that there will be a referendum on independence in 2014, in which sixteen and seventeen year olds will get the vote for the first time.

Elections

How do party volunteers help in election campaigns?

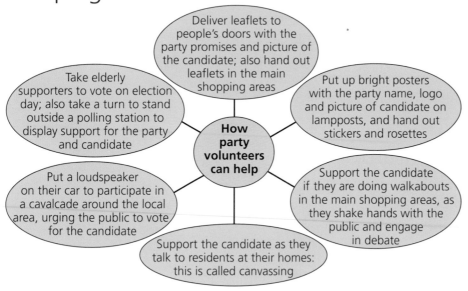

Figure 3.5 Ways in which party volunteers can help in election campaigns

Electoral systems

Proportional representation

The electoral system used for the Scottish parliament and Scottish local authority elections is called Proportional Representation (PR). In a PR system, there is a more direct link between the number of votes received and the number of seats won. For the Scottish parliament elections the PR system used is called the Additional Member System (AMS). For the Scottish local authority elections the Single Transferable Vote (STV) system is used.

Arguments in favour of proportional representation

- PR is 'fair' because it produces a close correlation between the share of votes and the share of seats. In the Scottish parliament elections in 2011 the Conservatives won about 13% of the votes and about 12% of the seats.
- PR can give minority parties more parliamentary representation. In the 2003 elections for the Scottish parliament the AMS system enabled the Scottish Socialist Party, the Green Party, the Scottish Senior Citizens Unity Party and the Independents to be represented.
- It is argued that PR will reduce the number of 'wasted votes' and so encourage greater voter turnout.

> **Hints & tips** ★
>
> *You may be asked about the advantages or disadvantages of proportional representation electoral systems. It is important that you try to include examples in your answer if you wish to gain full marks.*

Arguments against proportional representation

- PR can create a government in which a minority party can implement its policies. The Liberal Democrats finished fourth in the 2003 Scottish election, yet formed a government with Labour.
- It can lead to an unstable and weak government. The minority SNP Government of 2007–11 found it difficult to implement its policies. It failed, for example, to implement its policy of minimum pricing of alcohol in November 2010.
- It can lead to extremist parties gaining representation. In the 2009 European elections, the British National Party (BNP) won two seats.

Additional Member System

The Scottish parliament, Welsh assembly and London assembly are all elected using the Additional Member System (AMS). The system is a mixture of First Past the Post (FPTP) and PR. In Scotland voters cast two votes.

- The first vote uses FPTP to elect the 73 winning candidates in the local constituency elections.
- The second vote allows voters to choose between parties in a multi-member constituency. The country is divided into eight regional lists and each region elects seven regional list MSPs.

The 56 regional list MSPs are added to the 73 constituency MSPs to give a total of 129 MSPs in the Scottish parliament.

Until the 2011 Scottish Parliament election no party had won a majority of seats. This led to the creation of Labour and Liberal Democrat Coalition Governments after the 1999 and 2003 elections and a minority SNP Government after the 2007 election.

Single Transferable Vote

Local councils in Scotland are elected using the Single Transferrable Vote (STV) system. The system was first used in May 2007. This PR system results in a fairer distribution of seats across the parties but it can also mean that no one party has a majority. As a result, fewer councils are controlled by a single party. The main features of STV are given below.

- In multi-member constituencies (where more than one representative is elected in a constituency) voters rank the candidates in order of preference. So in a constituency with four representatives, voters will rank the candidates using the numbers 1–4.
- There will often be more candidates standing in the election than there are seats to be filled; the number of candidates will often be in double figures. Electors can vote for as many or as few candidates as they like.
- A quota system is used to calculate the minimum number of votes required to win one of the seats to be filled.

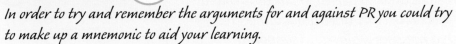

Hints & tips

In order to try and remember the arguments for and against PR you could try to make up a mnemonic to aid your learning.

For example, the arguments **for** could be: *C.L.E.N.*

✓ *Coalition — more likely to result in coalitions so more people are represented in government.*

✓ *Link — closer link between percentage of votes and percentage of seats.*

✓ *Encourage — under PR there are fewer wasted votes so it is supposed to encourage turnout.*

✓ *Normal — other countries use it, like Germany.*

See if you can make one up of your own for the arguments against.

Voter turnout

There has been a serious decline in voter turnout in Scottish elections, especially among young people. In the 1999 Scottish Parliament elections, 58.2% of those eligible turned out to vote. The 2011 election saw a reduced turnout of 50.2%. This is explained by **voter apathy**. It is clear that many citizens are dissatisfied with the political parties.

Key words

Voter apathy: A lack of interest or engagement in the political process.

Questions and model answers

Describe question

Political parties' campaign to get their candidates elected as councillors in a number of ways.

Describe, **in detail**, **two** ways in which political parties campaign to get their candidates elected as councillors.   **4 marks**

Model answer

Political parties campaign to get their candidates elected in number of different ways. One way is to canvass voters. Parties will employ a number of volunteers who will work alongside the candidates as they go door-to-door or even telephone households. They canvass voters by discussing the election with them in person and in doing so try to gain their vote.

Another way political parties help in election campaigns is by producing a large variety of promotional materials. These may take the form of leaflets that are delivered through the doors of voters and even huge billboard posters in town centres such as Falkirk to promote their candidates for the local authority. For example, in many council ⇨

Remember

Knowledge questions will have four, six or eight marks allocated and you will need to answer two questions — one describe question and one explain question.

wards during elections, lampposts are usually covered in placards with a candidate's name on them and quite often cars drive around the streets with loudspeakers through which a message is played to support a campaign.

Marker's comments

This is a very good answer because it is both relevant and detailed. Each point is fully explained, with examples from local council elections where possible. Each paragraph clearly includes at least one point that addresses the question and the candidate is showing clearly that they understand the question completely. This answer would gain full marks.

4 marks

Explain question ❓

The Additional Member System (AMS) is used to elect MSPs to the Scottish parliament. There are advantages and disadvantages to the system.

Explain, **in detail**, the advantages and disadvantages of AMS. **8 marks**

Model answer

The AMS voting system has been used in the Scottish parliament election system since 1999. One advantage of AMS is that it is a proportional representation system so there will be a closer link between the share of votes and the share of the seats. For example, in the 2011 Scottish Parliament election the Scottish Conservatives gained 13% of the votes and 12% of the seats. This is seen by many as being 'fairer' to the voters, as the number of MSPs will reflect each party's popularity.

Another advantage of the system is the greater choice it offers voters. Under AMS, voters cast a vote on two ballot papers. One vote is for a constituency MSP and the other is for a regional MSP. On the first paper they will vote for an individual MSP and on the second they will vote for a party. By doing this, smaller parties such as the Greens gain representation in the parliament.

However, having two MSPs creates a disadvantage as it creates a two-tier system of MSPs. Constituency MSPs, such as Nicola Sturgeon, have been directly elected by their constituency residents and so there will be a strong link between the representative and the people in the constituency. However, the people of Glasgow Southside who voted for Nicola Sturgeon also have seven regional MSPs that have been chosen by the political parties. It is thought that the link between constituents and this type of MSP is not so strong.

Remember

In an explain question, up to four marks can be awarded for each explanation you make, depending on their quality, level of detail, relevance, accuracy and exemplification.

Another disadvantage of AMS is that it usually results in a coalition government. A Labour–Liberal Democrat Coalition Government led the Scottish parliament between 1999 and 2007. Many people see this as a disadvantage because the government's policies have to be renegotiated after the election and so the original manifesto promises are sometimes not carried out. Another criticism is that AMS can give a political party more power than it is entitled to based on the number of votes it received. For example, in 2003 the Liberal Democrats came fourth in the election but they formed a coalition government with the Labour Party and had a huge influence over the way the country was run. The SNP and the Conservatives actually had more public support than the Liberal Democrats but they ended up with less power in the Parliament.

Marker's comments

This answer is a brilliant example as it clearly addresses the question. It looks at four separate arguments and provides excellent and up-to-date examples to help enhance the response. The candidate shows his or her deeper knowledge by including examples of current politicians and election results. The answer also provides both advantages and disadvantages, giving it balance. Due to the detail and exemplification, each of the paragraphs is worth four marks. As the maximum number of marks available is eight, the answer would be awarded 8/8.

8 marks

The House of Commons

All of the MPs elected in the general election work within the House of Commons. The House of Commons operates on the principle of debate and therefore is an **adversarial system**. Members of the governing party sit on one side of the chamber and the opposition parties sit on the other side.

Legislation	All MPs are involved in making laws and discussing and amending Bills.
Committees	Selected MPs will be on committees that look in detail at proposed legislation and government departments.
Scrutinising the work of the government	All MPs question the work of the government and debate relevant issues.

Table 4.3 The work of the House of Commons

Roles within the UK parliament

Prime minister

Figure 4.1 The current Prime Minister David Cameron

The prime minister is the leader of the governing party. As in the Scottish parliament, in most cases this will be the party with the most seats in the House of Commons. The current UK government is a **coalition**, which means that power is shared between parties, in this case Conservative and Liberal Democrat (see coalition government on page 28). **Party whips** perform the same role in the UK parliament as they do in the Scottish parliament and government MPs usually obey the prime minister's wishes. The prime minister appoints whom he wants to the **cabinet (power of patronage)** and it is in the interests of MPs to support their party leader if they want to be given a role in the cabinet. Like the first minister in Scotland, the prime minister is the public face of the government.

The prime minister appoints MPs and peers from his or her party to run government departments. There is a government department to look after each of the devolved and reserved powers listed in Table 3.3. Two of the most powerful positions in the UK cabinet are the chancellor of the exchequer, who is in charge of government finances and taxation, and the foreign secretary.

Key words

Adversarial system: A relationship in which two or more organisations oppose each other.

Coalition government: When two or more political parties form a government to run the country.

Party whip: The party whip is appointed by the leadership of a political party to persuade or pressurise MSPs into supporting the party – this is called following the party line.

Power of patronage: The power to appoint or remove individuals from office.

Remember

Cabinet ministers are not responsible for devolved powers. For instance, education and health ministers are only in charge of education and health services in England.

Remember

Party	Number of seats	Percentage of seats	
Conservatives	307	47.3	Coalition government 59%
Liberal Democrats	57	8.7	
Labour	258	39.7	Opposition 41%
Other	28	4.3	
Total	650	100	100

Table 4.4 2010 general election results

Hints & tips ★

The present UK government is a coalition. Make sure you know at least two or three members of the UK government. Visit www.number10.gov.uk/the-coalition/the-cabinet.

Leader of the opposition

The current leader of the opposition is the Labour leader, Ed Milliband. This is a high profile position and the leader of the opposition receives a lot of media attention. They are seen as the chief critic of the government and although they do not have any direct power within the House of Commons, they can have a big influence in the popularity of the government. The opposition party selects its own MPs to form a **shadow cabinet**, which scrutinises the policies and decisions of the government.

How representative is the House of Commons?

Ethnic minorities and women are not well represented in the UK parliament.

The UK ethnic minority population is around 16% but the results from the 2010 general election show that only around 4.2% of MPs are from a non-white background.

Similarly, 22% of MPs are female (144 out of 650), whereas 51% of the UK population is female.

Reasons for the poor representation of ethnic minorities and women are thought to include:
- The working hours of the UK parliament often results in women with families being put off becoming MPs.
- There are no crèche facilities in the Palace of Westminster.
- There is a white male culture within the House of Commons.
- Political parties do not select enough women and ethnic minority candidates for elections.

Hints & tips ★

Make sure you study the work of an MP in parliament as this will also enhance your knowledge of the House of Commons (see page 24).

The House of Lords

The House of Lords, also known as the Second Chamber or Upper House, is an appointed chamber – members are not elected by the public. They play an advisory role in parliament – they are not involved in running the country on a day-to-day basis but they can still have a lot of influence in the law-making process. The people who sit in the House of Lords are called peers and they have the title Lord or Baroness.

Legislation	All Bills are debated in the House of Lords before they become law.
Committees	Some peers are appointed because they have experience in a specific area. They then sit on committees that look into relevant matters.
Scrutinising the work of the government	Government matters are questioned and debated in the House of Lords.

Table 4.5 The work of the House of Lords

How does the Lords affect decision making?

Many people believe the House of Lords to be an important part of the UK parliament for the following reasons:

- Through the work of committees they can amend Bills passing through parliament.
- Many Lords are experts in a particular field and can offer sound advice on new legislation.
- The Lords can potentially delay non-financial Bills by up to one year.
- By disagreeing with the government they may be able to force a rethink on policy.

How are Lords appointed?

The vast majority of members of the House of Lords are **life peers** – people who have been selected by governments (over the years) due to their expertise in specific fields. In contrast, **hereditary peers** are people who have inherited a title from someone in their family. The number of hereditary peers was reduced substantially after reforms in 1999 and the current hereditary peers are now unable to pass on their titles. There are also a small number of **Lords spiritual**, who are bishops from the Church of England.

Once a Lord accepts his or her place in the House of Lords the appointment is for the rest of their life (but cannot be passed on to their descendants).

Issues with the House of Lords

A common theme within recent politics has been reform of the House of Lords. Many people feel that as the House of Lords is an unelected chamber it is not democratic. Many governments have tried to reform the role of the chamber.

House of Lords Act 1999

This Act reduced the number of hereditary peers in the House of Lords to 92 and by July 2012 there were only 89 hereditary peers. Since 1999 many governments have tried to reform the House of Lords further but largely without success. However, in 2009 the UK Court of Appeal – the highest appeal court in the UK – was moved from the House of Lords to the UK Supreme Court.

House of Lords Reform Bill 2012

In 2012, the Coalition Government recommended that the number of peers be reduced from 826 to 450 and that 80% of members should be elected rather than appointed. They also recommended that the number of Church of England bishops be reduced and that a time limit on the term to be served be introduced. Peers would no longer be members for life but would serve a non-renewable fifteen-year term instead. The Bill did not make it through parliament because there was not enough support from backbench Conservative MPs.

Differences between the House of Commons and the House of Lords

House of Commons	House of Lords
Elected MPs.	Appointed peers.
MPs can be from any background and have any qualifications.	Most peers are appointed due to their expertise in a specific field.
MPs have to win an election every five years.	Once appointed, Lords and Baronesses have the position for life.
MPs are paid a salary plus expenses.	Peers receive only an allowance and expenses.
MPs represent constituents.	Peers represent only themselves.
Nearly all MPs are members of a political party.	Many peers are members of a political party but a large number are not.

Table 4.6 Differences between the two Houses of Parliament

Participation

There are three main political parties in the UK: the Conservatives, Labour and the Liberal Democrats. There are also smaller parties including the Green Party and the UK Independence Party.

What do political parties do?

Most MPs and Lords within the UK parliament are affiliated with political parties. Once elected, MPs connected to a political party are expected to represent the policies of the party. If an MP does not do this they can be removed from the party and will not have the party's support at the next general election.

Before an election, political parties will create their own ideas of how, if elected, they will try to improve the country. These ideas are known as **policies**. As part of the election campaign, the parties will collate these ideas in their **party manifestos**, which voters and the media can read.

The aim of a political party is to win as many seats as possible in an election. The more seats they win, the greater the influence the party will have in how the country is run and the easier it will be for them to put their policies into action.

Key words

Party manifesto: A party publication which contains the policies they hope to implement, if elected.

Political parties in the UK and their policies

Political party	Conservatives	Labour	Liberal Democrats
Leader in 2013	David Cameron	Ed Milliband	Nick Clegg
	Conservatives	Labour	LIBERAL DEMOCRATS
Key policies	• To reduce the UK's deficit drastically within five years. • To create the 'Big Society': encouraging charities, voluntary groups and cooperatives to provide local services.	• To reduce the UK's deficit but protect frontline services such as the NHS, schools and policing. • To replace Trident to maintain the UK's nuclear deterrent.	• To reform the voting system and push for a referendum to end First Past the Post in the general elections. • To maintain the UK's position within the European Union.

Table 4.7 Political parties in the UK and their policies

Coalition Government

After the 2010 general election, there was no political party with an outright majority of seats within the House of Commons. The Conservatives and Liberal Democrats decided to form a coalition of both parties to run the country. As a result some Liberal Democrat policies, such as holding a referendum on the voting system, and some Conservative policies, such as increasing university fees in England and Wales, were brought together in a 'Coalition Agreement'.

Some people argue that the Coalition Government is unfair because voters did not vote for the combined policies of the Coalition Agreement. The Labour Party had won 258 seats in the election yet has no role in the government (and therefore little power in parliament), but the Liberal Democrats, having come third in the election with 57 seats, are now in a more powerful position to influence legislation. However, the two parties in the Coalition Government gained a combined 59% of the votes in the election and so they have a right to govern and can form a strong and stable government.

Elections

What role do political parties play in election campaigns?

Political parties co-ordinate election campaigns in the weeks and months before a general election or a by-election (held when an MP retires, resigns or dies in the period between general elections).

Political parties invest large amounts of money trying to get their candidates elected. Some of this money is spent on designing and printing posters and leaflets to help promote a candidate.

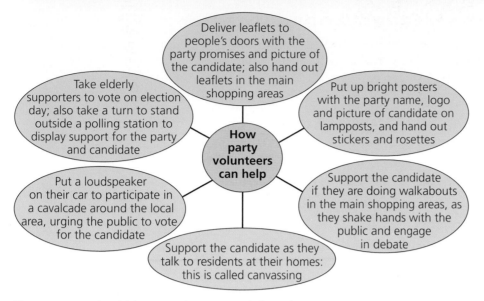

Figure 4.2 Ways in which party volunteers can help in election campaigns

Electoral system

First Past the Post

In a general election, each of the 650 constituencies in the UK elects one member of parliament (MP). The candidate who wins the most votes in a constituency becomes the MP. The electoral system used to elect members to the UK parliament is called First Past the Post (FPTP). This is a simple majority system – sometimes called the winner-takes-all system.

Advantages of FPTP

- It usually provides a strong single-party government and allows the prime minister and the cabinet to pursue policies clearly stated in their election manifesto.
- The system prevents extremist parties from obtaining representation. The British National Party (BNP) achieved over half a million votes in the 2010 general election but gained no seats.
- It is easy to understand and implement. Voters vote only once and the results are announced very quickly. In contrast there were 140 000 spoilt ballot papers in the 2007 Scottish Parliament elections, which was under a different electoral system.

Disadvantages of FPTP

- It does not always deliver a decisive victory for one party or create a strong and stable government. The Conservatives failed to gain an overall majority in the 2010 general election.
- It can lead to a situation where the winning MP in a constituency has received less than 30% of the vote. In 2010, the Labour candidate won the Hampstead and Kilburn seat with only 42 votes more than the Conservative candidate.

Remember

You may be asked about the advantages or disadvantages of First Past the Post electoral systems. It is important that you try to include examples in your answer if you wish to gain full marks.

- The number of seats in the House of Commons does not accurately reflect the percentages of votes for each of the parties. In 2010, the Liberal Democrats gained 23% of the votes but only 57 seats, while Labour gained 29% of the vote but 258 seats.

Hints & tips

*In order to try and remember the arguments for and against FPTP you could try to make up a mnemonic to aid your learning. For example, **B.E.E.S.***

✓ ***By-elections** – FPTP allows by-elections*

✓ ***Extremist** – the system prevents extremist parties*

✓ ***Easy** – FPTP is easy to understand and simple*

✓ ***Strong** – the system provides strong government*

Voter turnout

The number of people voting in UK elections has fallen since the end of the Second World War. The average turnout since that time has been 78% but in 2001 only 59.4% of those eligible to vote did so. The figure increased to 65% in 2010 but **voter apathy** is still considered a serious problem. Dissatisfaction with political parties and the 2009 MPs' expenses scandal are two of the reasons given to explain the low turnout. The decline in turnout is found particularly amongst young people.

Key words

Voter apathy: A lack of interest or engagement in the political process.

Questions and model answers

Hints & tips

Make sure you take account of how many marks a question is worth. You should base the length of your answers on the time you should allocate to four mark, six mark and eight mark questions.

Remember

Knowledge questions will have four, six or eight marks allocated and you will need to answer two questions – one describe question and one explain question.

Describe question

Political parties campaign to get their candidates elected as MPs in a number of ways.

Describe, **in detail**, at least two ways in which political parties campaign to get their candidates elected as MPs. **6 marks**

Model answer

Political parties campaign to get their candidates elected in number of different ways. One way is to canvass voters. Parties will employ a number of volunteers who will work alongside the candidates as they go door-to-door or even telephone households. They canvass voters by discussing the election with them in person and in doing so try to gain their vote.

Another way political parties help in election campaigns is by producing a large variety of promotional materials. This may take the form of leaflets that are delivered through the doors of voters and even huge billboard posters in town centres to promote their candidate. For example, in many constituencies during elections, lampposts are usually covered in placards with the candidate's name on them, and quite often cars drive around the streets with loudspeakers through which a message is played to support a campaign.

Political parties will also try to get candidates elected by orchestrating national campaigns to try to persuade voters and even certain groups of voters. Before the 2010 election, the Liberal Democrats had most of their candidates publically pledge to halt a rise in tuition fees within England and Wales. Political parties also use party political broadcasts on the television in which the party leader tries to persuade people to vote for their local candidates.

Marker's comment

This is a very good answer because it is relevant and detailed. Each point is fully explained with examples where possible. Each paragraph clearly includes at least one point that addresses the question and the candidate is showing clearly that they understand the question completely. This answer would gain full marks. **6 marks**

Shop stewards

Shop stewards (also called union representatives) are elected by the union members in a workplace. In the same way that an MP represents the people in a constituency, a union shop steward represents the members of the union and will listen to their concerns and work with the employer to try to resolve them. The shop steward will represent their union members at regional and national meetings of the trade union.

The methods used by trade unions

Trade unions use negotiation to try to change working practices for their members, such as securing better pay deals or improving the working environment. If negotiation fails, they can use a number of forms of industrial action to try to put pressure on an employer to meet their demands. Union members must be balloted before any industrial action can take place, and action can only take place if a majority of those who vote are in favour of it.

Industrial action	What it means
Overtime ban	Members will only work their contracted number of hours.
Go slow	Members will deliberately take more time to do their job and will not attempt to be overly productive.
Work-to-rule	Members will not perform any duties over and above those stated in their contract of employment.
Strike	Members refuse to work in order to put pressure on their employer. This is the most serious action that union members can take. Members will not be paid by the employer during the period of the strike. The threat of a strike can sometimes be enough to gain concessions from an employer.

Table 5.1 Forms of industrial action

Rights and responsibilities of trade unions

Rights

- To take industrial action.
- To recruit new members.
- To be consulted about changes to working conditions by employers.
- To ask about changes to pay and working conditions.

Responsibilities

- To follow the legal procedures and to ensure protests are peaceful.
- Not to force or bully people into joining.

- To ensure they act with their members' consent and do not act in their own interests.
- Not to make unreasonable demands or threaten employers.

Example 1: UK

Firefighters vote over strike action

In autumn 2013, firefighters in parts of the UK walked out for four hours with the threat of further action. Firefighters are taking issue over government proposals that they will have to work more years before they can receive their pensions.

Example 2: Scotland

Train drivers in strike vote over 6.4% pay rise

In October 2013, ASLEF, the train drivers' union, held a ballot on industrial action. The conflict revolved around pay demands and changes to drivers' shift patterns. A 'yes' vote to ban overtime would mean no Sunday services at all for the whole of Scotland.

Pressure groups

A pressure group is a group of people who work together to try to influence public opinion and government policy on a particular issue. There are thousands of pressure groups in the UK working on a range of causes, including human rights, food, animal welfare and the environment. Some pressure groups are large international organisations; others are small, local campaigns, such as a protest over plans to close a school.

The aims of pressure groups

Some pressure groups will have a single aim; others will have several aims, but they are always directly related to the issue involved. The North Kelvin Meadow Campaign is a community group in the West End of Glasgow that campaigns for an area of green space near Maryhill to be retained as a multi-use community area. In contrast, the Countryside Alliance works on a range of issues, including the promotion of hunting, shooting and rural life.

There are two types of pressure group: cause groups and sectional groups. Cause (or promotional) pressure groups promote a particular cause, while sectional pressure groups represent the interests of a group or section of society.

Cause groups	Sectional groups
Membership is open to anyone who supports the cause.	Membership is restricted to the people whose interests the group represents, such as teachers or nurses.
Groups may be small and may be temporary – they may only exist for as long as the cause exists. Others may have been established for a long time and may have a huge membership. Some of these groups are registered charities.	Groups are well organised and campaign on the issues that affect their members. They can threaten industrial action in order to achieve their aims.
Examples: **Greenpeace** – campaigns on a global scale on environmental issues. **Amnesty International** – a multi-national group that campaigns for human rights.	Examples: **BMA (British Medical Association)** – represents the interests of doctors. **Unison** – the UK's largest public sector worker trade union, which represents NHS staff and civil servants.

Table 5.2 Cause and sectional pressure groups

The methods used by pressure groups

Contact representatives	Pressure groups: • contact their representatives, for example MPs, MSPs or councillors, to draw attention to the subject • ask for support and public acknowledgement of support by backing a campaign • try to persuade the representative to vote the preferred way in parliament over the subject.
Draw up petitions	Pressure groups often draw up petitions to gain public support in order to show that members of the public have strong feelings about the issue. Petitions are often signed in public areas, such as town centres, or can be supported through online petitions or social media such as Facebook and Twitter.
Organise public protests	Pressure groups often organise public protests to support their causes and these can be marches, demonstrations or rallies. Public protests generally make the local or national news and are a good way of getting attention for the issue.
Create campaigns to suit the issue	Pressure groups use different styles of campaign to gain support, depending on the type of issue: • leaflets can be posted through letter boxes in residential areas or handed out in public areas • posters can be displayed in appropriate areas • the Internet, and social media such as Facebook and Twitter, is used by such pressure groups as Amnesty International.
Mass media	Pressure groups use mass media, such as newspapers, television and radio, to promote their causes. • News items or advertisements can be placed in newspapers or magazines to promote the issue and gain support. • Guests could appear on television or radio programmes, or as panellists on current events or news programmes.

Table 5.3 Methods used by pressure groups

Rights and responsibilities of pressure groups

Rights

- To protest, through marches, demonstrations and industrial action.
- To promote their cause using mass media and new media.
- To actively try to recruit new members.
- To contact representatives to try to gain their support.
- To organise petitions to show public support.

Responsibilities

- To protest legally and peacefully.
- Not to slander individuals or tell lies in order to try to persuade people to support the cause.
- Not to force people to join the group, or bully or intimidate people who oppose their aims.
- Not to intimidate politicians, or threaten blackmail to further their cause.
- Not to falsify signatures. Support for the cause must be genuine.

Example 1: UK

UK Uncut

UK Uncut is a pressure group aiming to highlight alternatives to the Conservative–Liberal Democrat spending cuts. The group uses direct action to get its message across, often closing down high street stores they believe are owned by tax avoiders. In December 2012, they targeted scores of Starbucks coffee shops across Britain as they sought to highlight the chain's minimal contributions to the UK exchequer.

Example 2: Scotland

Campaign launched to prevent closure of post offices

In October 2013, Scottish Sub-Postmasters have begun a campaign to prevent the closure of hundreds of post offices. Customers will be asked to sign special campaign postcards, to be sent to their local MSPs and also to sign a national petition.

The media

Media is the different ways that information is communicated to the public and includes newspapers (print media), radio and television (broadcast media) and the Internet (new media). Today, social media is another important means of communication of news and information.

The media has three roles in society:
- to entertain
- to educate
- to inform.

By controlling the information that is communicated, the media can shape our attitudes and opinions. The UK has a **free press**, which means that the media can criticise the government and political parties, and politicians will aim to keep the media 'on their side' so that they do not receive negative press coverage.

Newspapers

Newspapers are classified as 'tabloids' (such as the *Mail*, and the *Daily Record*) or 'broadsheets' (such as the *Telegraph* and the *Herald*).

Most newspapers favour a particular political party and the stories that they print will tend to reflect favourably on that party. For example, the *Mail* is known to support the Conservative Party and will print stories that show David Cameron in a positive light. At the same time, they will print stories that show the other political parties in a bad light. In this way newspapers can shape our attitudes and opinions about political parties and can encourage us to vote for a particular party in an election.

Newspapers and elections

Politicians understand the importance of having the support of the media. Over 12 million people buy a newspaper every day in the UK – that is a lot of potential voters that a newspaper can influence.

In 1992, the *Sun*, Britain's biggest selling daily newspaper, gave its support to the Conservative Party and when the Conservatives won the general election the newspaper declared 'It's the Sun wot won it'. The newspaper switched to support the Labour Party in the 1997 election and declared 'The Sun backs Blair', but in the run up to the 2010 election it returned to support the Conservatives, announcing 'Labour's lost it.' Other national newspapers also moved their support from the Labour Party, who went on to lose power to the Conservatives.

In Scotland, the SNP did not have the full support of any national newspaper before the 2007 Scottish Parliament elections. The party won the election but only won enough votes to form a minority government. In the run up to the 2011 election the party gained the backing of the *Scottish Sun* newspaper and this time won enough votes in the election to form a majority government.

The overall influence of newspapers should not be exaggerated but the evidence shows that having the support of a major national newspaper does not harm a party at election time.

Television

While newspapers can support a political party, broadcast media – television and radio – must follow strict broadcasting guidelines and remain **politically impartial**. There is an independent body, called Ofcom, responsible for making sure that television channels are not biased towards any political party or agenda and that their reporting is neutral.

Television and elections

The run up to the 2010 general election was the first time that televised leaders' debates had taken place in the UK. (This is a common occurrence during election campaigns in the USA.) The leaders of the three main parties – Nick Clegg (Liberal Democrats), David Cameron (Conservatives) and Gordon Brown (Labour) – took part in three debates broadcast, in turn, by ITV, BSkyB and the BBC.

Figure 5.2 The 2010 televised leaders' debates

Nick Clegg came across most favourably in the debates, ahead of both of the other leaders, and support for the Liberal Democrats increased considerably in the run up to polling day. The party increased their share of the vote in the election but ultimately lost seats.

Televised debates were also held in Scotland for the first time in the run up to the 2011 Scottish Parliament elections. The leaders of the four main parties took part in the debates – Alex Salmond (SNP), Iain Gray (Labour), Annabel Goldie (Conservatives) and Tavish Scott (Liberal Democrats).

Unlike the UK debates, these debates did not appear to have a significant impact on public opinion in the run up to polling day, though Alex Salmond appeared to come across most favourably during the events, while the other leaders failed to capitalise on the opportunity.

New media and the Internet

The Internet and social media now play a major role in the communication of information. Like newspapers, websites are not required to be politically impartial and they can show support for a particular party. Political parties use their websites and social media pages to engage voters (particularly younger voters) and generate support.

Activities

Research how a political party might use social media during an election campaign.

Control of the media

The Press Complaints Commission (PCC) is an independent body that deals with complaints about things written in newspapers and magazines. Journalists and newspapers must follow its **code of practice** and not publish incorrect or misleading information about people, companies, groups or political parties.

> **Key words**
>
> **Code of practice:** A set of guidelines that must be followed, e.g. for newspapers on acceptable reporting.

Leveson Inquiry

In 2012, an independent enquiry (called the Leveson Inquiry) was held into the freedom of the press. The inquiry was the result of allegations of phone hacking of celebrities and members of the public by the (now defunct) *News of the World* newspaper. Following the inquiry, a cross-party agreement for a Royal Charter was announced in early 2013. The charter will protect the freedom of the press and at the same time protect the public from the kinds of abuses that made the Leveson Inquiry necessary. There will be a new independent self-regulatory body that will deal fairly with complaints and ensure that newspapers print apologies on their front page if they publish statements that are proven to be inaccurate. The body will be able to mount investigations and, where appropriate, impose meaningful sanctions on inaccurate reporting.

Who owns the media?

The BBC is paid for by a licence fee that everyone in the UK must pay if they own a television. BSkyB is owned by several shareholders, including Rupert Murdoch (39%). Rupert Murdoch's News Corporation company also owns the *Sun* and *The Times* newspapers, which means he has a lot of influence over the media in the UK.

Part Three: Social Issues in the UK

This section of the book provides summary course notes for the Social Issues in the UK unit of the course.

You will have studied one of the following topics as part of your National 5 Social Issues unit:

- Social Inequality, or
- Crime and the Law.

In the knowledge section of the exam you will answer **one describe question** and **one explain question** on this unit and these questions will be allocated four, six or eight marks each.

Low pay

- Having a job is not always enough to escape severe poverty, because some jobs, especially part-time and unskilled jobs, are low paid.
- As a result those who are low paid can find themselves just above, or even just below, the poverty line. They therefore have to rely on benefits to make ends meet.

Benefits system

- Families in severe poverty are more likely to be claiming benefits and tax credits and many employed people need state benefits just to get by.
- These benefits cost the government billions of pounds every year.
- The Conservative–Liberal Democrat Coalition Government introduced the means testing of child benefit in 2013 and there are calls for more benefits to be **means tested** in order to reduce the amount the government pays out. Some arguments for and against are below.

Arguments in favour of more means testing of benefits	Arguments against more means testing of benefits
Some of the people who currently receive state benefits do not really need them.	People in need are not always aware that they are entitled to benefits.
Benefits should be paid to the people who need them the most, not to everyone regardless of their level of need.	People are embarrassed to claim benefits because of the stigma attached to means testing.
When government budgets are being cut, it is sensible to reduce unnecessary benefits payments and use the money where it is needed more.	People who have contributed to the welfare system should not be denied access to benefits when they are entitled to them.

Table 6.2

Family structure

- Families with children are more likely to experience poverty than those without.
- When a child is born, the family income usually drops because the parent(s) need to reduce their hours of work or pay for childcare.
- Children living with parents who are under 25 are more likely to be in severe poverty than children who live with older parents.

Gender

- In Scotland, more than half of those in low-paid work (work that pays less than £7 per hour) are part-time workers and the great majority of them are women. Women account for two-thirds of all low-paid workers in Scotland.
- On average, women in the UK earn about 15% less than men.
- Jobs that are traditionally done by women, such as nursing, are usually less well paid than jobs traditionally done by men, such as engineering.
- Women tend to be responsible for most of the childcare in a family and it can be difficult to fit this in around a paid job. Some employers may be less likely to hire a woman of childbearing age in case they fall pregnant (and therefore need time off work).

Key words

Means tests: A way of checking if a person has enough income or financial resources to support themselves. The result of the test will determine if they are entitled to receive certain state benefits.

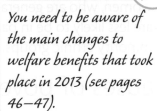
Hints & tips

You need to be aware of the main changes to welfare benefits that took place in 2013 (see pages 46–47).

Race

- There is a strong link between ethnicity and low pay or income poverty.
- 25% of black African, Bangladeshi and black Caribbean working-age households are not in work. This is compared to 10% of Indian working-age households and 15% of white working-age households.
- Almost 50% of all Bangladeshi and Pakistani employees are in low-paid work (work that pays less than £7 per hour).
- Around a third of Bangladeshis and Pakistanis are unemployed but say they do not want to work. This figure is much higher than for other ethnic groups.

The consequences of poverty

Physical consequences and ill health

Children who grow up in poverty suffer more health problems than children who grow up under better financial circumstances. Many infants born into poverty have a low birth weight, which is associated with many preventable mental and physical disabilities.

Inequality in education

There is a link between growing up in poverty and educational underachievement. Children who grow up in poverty are more likely to do less well at school than their classmates. On average, there is a 60% gap in attainment levels at S4 between children living in low-income households and their better-off classmates.

Education is a key factor in determining the likelihood of experiencing poverty. The lower a person's qualifications, the more likely they are to be unemployed and if they have a job the more likely they are to be in low-paid work.

Social exclusion

Parents living in severe poverty often cannot afford childcare. Because of the high cost of childcare, many parents often have to give up work or turn down a job. For them, work does not pay, trapping them and their children in poverty. Families living on a low income generally have to go without certain essential items.

Poor housing

Children living in poor housing are at a higher risk of ill health and disability. They can lose out on vital schooling, endure mental and physical ill health and fall into a cycle of social exclusion and poverty.

Addiction problems

Social exclusion and poverty can lead some people to become addicted to alcohol or drugs. People who feel trapped in a cycle of poverty and deprivation are more likely to turn to alcohol or drugs to help them feel better.

Groups that can help to tackle poverty

The Welfare State

In the UK, the **Welfare State** has the responsibility to protect the health and wellbeing of its citizens, especially those in financial or social need, by ensuring that everyone has a minimum standard of living.

Support for children

The main benefits for children are **child benefit** and **child tax credit**. Most people living in the UK can claim child benefit for their children.

Some children are entitled to free school meals or help with the costs of school uniform. Vouchers to help with the cost of milk, fruit or vegetables may be available if the parent is pregnant or has young children.

Far-reaching changes are currently being made to welfare provision. Some of the key welfare reforms in 2013 are outlined below.

Key words

Welfare State: Where the state plays a major role in looking after the wellbeing of its citizens.

January	• Sliding cuts to child benefit if one parent earns £50,000 or more. Child benefit ends if one parent earns more than £60,000.
April	• Housing benefit cut to reflect house size and 'over-occupation': there will be a 14% cut for a house with one spare bedroom and a 25% cut for two or more extra bedrooms. Around 80,000 claimants in Scotland are expected to lose an average of £12 per week. Claimants' options include paying the difference, moving home or taking in a lodger. This change is being called the 'bedroom tax'.
	• Phased replacement of Disability Living Allowance (DLA) with personal independent payments, involving a cut of around 20% (around £260 million in Scotland). An estimated 55,000 people in Scotland are expected to lose DLA.
	• An overall housing benefits cap to be imposed of £500 per week for couples and £350 per week for single people.
October	• Phased introduction of the Universal Credit, which will gradually replace housing benefit, tax credits and out-of-work benefits. Paid directly to claimants, not landlords, each month, leading to fears of increased homelessness through rent arrears and bad debts.

Source: Audit Scotland Welfare Reforms Update, November 2012 and the *Sunday Herald*, 6 January 2013

Table 6.3

The future of the Welfare State

Large spending cuts of £81 billion between 2010 and 2015 have been announced by the coalition government, caused by the recession of 2008. The Scottish government will receive around £3 billion less in its allocation from the UK Treasury for the period 2012–16 and this will have an effect on all government spending, including welfare. As a result of this, welfare is moving away from the state and towards the individual, and social inequalities are widening.

From 2013 a **Universal Credit** will be introduced, which combines all welfare benefits into one payment. The idea is to simplify the system and allow people to manage their own finances. For example, rent payments will be made directly to the individual, who would then be responsible for paying the landlord or local authority at the required time.

Universal Credit

The new Universal Credit will simplify the benefits system by replacing separate payments for Jobseekers Allowance, Employment Support Allowance, Housing Benefit, Working Tax Credits and Child Tax Credit with one monthly payment. Money will be paid one month in arrears and the government admits that about 3 million families will see a reduction in their entitlement. The government hopes to reduce the welfare budget by £28 billion.

Attracting jobs to the UK

The government has to ensure that the UK remains attractive to companies around the globe. Firms have to believe that if they come to the UK, they will grow and succeed.

Training, education and Welfare to Work

The Youth Contract

A Youth Contract has been introduced by central government, which aims to tackle youth unemployment by helping young unemployed people to get a job.

Work experience

Included in the Youth Contract is the work experience scheme, which is voluntary and aims to help 16–24 year olds to find a job after a work placement.

Work Programme

The Work Programme is the central government's scheme to help the long-term unemployed, and those at risk of becoming long-term unemployed. The Work Programme providers include private companies and the public and voluntary sectors.

Support for NEETS

NEETS (those 'Not in Education, Employment or Training') are also supported through the Youth Contract. Providers help teenagers to move into full-time education, an apprenticeship or a job with training.

The minimum wage

All employers must pay their workers minimum hourly rates and these are set by the national minimum wage.

Activities

Use the Internet to find out about the national minimum wage.

Heating allowances

People who are unable to pay for their own heating needs, and who depend on long-term benefits, can claim a fuel allowance, which is a means-tested payment under the National Fuel Scheme to help with the cost of heating the home.

The **Winter Fuel Payment** is a universal benefit in the form of an annual payment, given to all UK citizens who are 60 and above to help with their winter fuel bills.

A **Cold Weather Payment** can also be paid to those in need when the local temperature is either recorded as, or forecast to be, an average of zero degrees Celsius or below over seven consecutive days. This benefit is means-tested.

The 'Big Society'

The Big Society describes the shift of power from central government to communities, volunteers and charities or non-profit groups, with these groups taking over the running of some public services.

Scottish parliament

Employment and training

The Scottish government is attempting to tackle child poverty by ensuring that people have the skills for the jobs that are available.

Opportunities for All

Opportunities for All offers all 16–19-year-old NEETS a place in learning or training.

The Employer Recruitment Incentive

This initiative helps small- and medium-sized businesses to employ a person aged eighteen or over who has been unemployed for six months or more.

Small Business Employment Support Fund

This fund assists small businesses to recruit staff.

Help for those on low pay

There are a range of measures the Scottish government has taken in this area. The Scottish government has funded initiatives that work with people to ensure that they receive the benefits to which they are entitled.

The Scottish Living Wage

The Living Wage aims to help reduce inequality and tackle 'in work' poverty, which affects around 20% of all workers in Scotland.

Education Maintenance Allowance (EMA)

The Education Maintenance Allowance allows many young people from low-paid households to remain in education. A good education is extremely important for a young person to succeed in later life. If you are 16–19 years old, in a school or college and come from a low-income family, you can apply for EMA. The allowance is means-tested and pays the student £30 per week. EMA has been scrapped in England by the Conservative–Liberal Democrat Coalition Government.

Help for young people to enter positive and sustained destinations

Community Jobs Scotland

Community Jobs Scotland helps long-term unemployed young people into employment.

Modern apprenticeships

Modern apprenticeships lead to employment opportunities and ensure that young people have the skills required for the jobs available.

One Parent Families

One Parent Families Scotland is a helpline that provides advice to single parents on a range of measures, such as access to childcare, accessing welfare benefits and employability advice.

Local employability partnerships

Local authorities and local employability partnerships work with young people to match training opportunities and other support with local labour market opportunities.

Community Planning Partnerships

Local authorities and Community Planning Partnerships support young people toward and into work.

Private sector

By creating employment opportunities private companies can help to reduce unemployment, which then helps to reduce poverty. They can also help by working with the government in public–private partnerships (PPP) to improve and regenerate public services, for example by funding the building of new hospitals and schools.

Health inequalities

The causes of health inequalities include both lifestyle choices, which people have some control over, and other environmental factors, over which people have little influence.

Remember

Welfare provision is the responsibility of the UK parliament. In contrast, health provision is the responsibility of the Scottish parliament.

Lifestyle choices

A person's lifestyle choices can have an effect on their health.

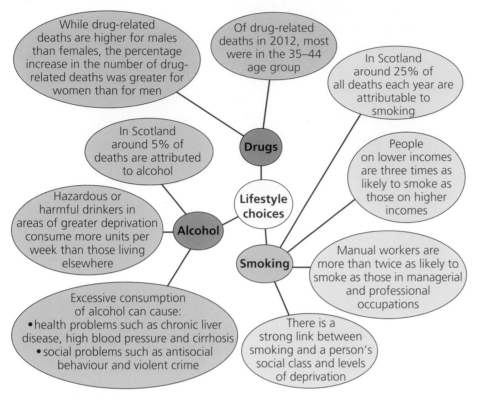

Figure 6.2 Lifestyle choices

Social and economic disadvantages

Overall life expectancy and healthy life expectancy is improving in Scotland. Yet despite this, the gap between rich and poor is widening. The poorest Scots are expected to die twenty years before the richest, with men in the most deprived areas having a life expectancy of 68, only one year above the retirement age.

In the most deprived parts of Scotland people are twice as likely to die of cancer before the age of 74 than those in the least deprived areas, and four times more likely to die of heart disease.

Figure 6.3 High-rise flats in Springburn, Glasgow

Geography and environment

A World Health Organization report found that in Glasgow there were serious health inequalities. The report states that a boy living in the deprived area of Calton had an average life expectancy of 54 years compared with a boy from Lenzie, a less deprived area 12 km away, who could expect to live to 82.

The 'Glasgow Effect' refers to people from socially deprived areas like Calton in Glasgow having a lower life expectancy and poorer health than people from similarly deprived parts of other cities in the UK, for example Liverpool and Manchester.

This effect highlights that shorter life expectancy in Scotland is not just due to factors such as alcohol, smoking, drug use, unemployment, housing and inequality but also where you live. Life expectancy is higher where deprivation is lower.

Age

- People living in rural areas, in general, live longer than those in towns.
- Men in the least deprived areas of Scotland may live 13.2 years longer than those in the most deprived areas, while women in the least deprived areas can expect to live 8.9 years longer than those in the most deprived.
- More babies born to mothers living in the most deprived areas have a low birth weight compared to those born to mothers living in the most affluent areas.
- There are large and increasing inequalities in the number of deaths among young adults due to drugs, alcohol, violence and suicide.

Mental health in later life

Depression is the most common mental health problem among the elderly, according to research by Age UK.

Dementia

Dementia can affect young people, although it is more common among older people. Figures from Alzheimer Scotland suggest that in 2013 the number of people with dementia who were under the age of 65 was around 2,300.

Minor problems of ageing

The term 'cumulative trivia' is given to the minor problems of ageing. Difficulties in being able to do straightforward tasks can make older people feel they are not coping or are becoming increasingly frail, and this can lead to depression. Older people often rely on health services to help maintain their independence and daily routines.

Gender issues

Scottish children have the lowest life expectancy within the UK, while English children have the highest. The average Scottish boy is expected to live to the age of 75.9, while an English boy will live to 78.6. Scottish girls are expected to live to the age of 80.4 years, which is 2.2 years less than English girls, who are expected to live to 82.6.

Race

Black and minority ethnic (BME) groups in the UK tend to have poorer health than white groups. However, there are also health inequalities between different BME groups, with some having worse health than others. BME groups as a whole are more likely to report ill health, and that often starts at a younger age than in the white British population.

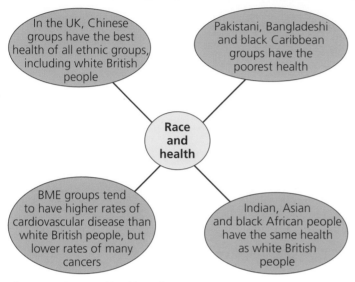

Figure 6.4 Race and health in the UK

Causes of ethnic health inequalities

Many BME groups experience higher rates of poverty than white British groups and this can lead to inequalities between and within BME groups. But there are other factors that cause health inequalities and these include racism and discrimination, the long-term impact of migration, differences in culture and lifestyles and access to health care.

- Men born in Asia are more likely to have heart problems.
- Men born in the Caribbean are more likely to die of a stroke.
- Cancer rates tend to be lower in BME groups.
- Asylum seekers suffer more from mental health problems.

Groups that try to tackle health inequalities

The Scottish parliament has primary and secondary legislative powers to run the National Health Service in Scotland.

The NHS in Scotland

People who live in Scotland are entitled to a wide range of health care from the National Health Service (NHS), including hospital treatments, doctors, dentists and opticians. Most health care provided by the NHS is free. However, it is also possible to access private health care, which can be paid for directly or through a private health care insurance scheme.

NHS24

NHS24 is a service that provides the public with health advice and information about illnesses and conditions, treatments, NHS services and other support services. It offers advice and information on how a person can look after their own and their family's health.

The private sector

Most people in Scotland who use private health care are still registered with an NHS GP. They may choose to access private health care when they are referred for specialist treatment or for an operation. Some employers offer membership of private schemes (such as BUPA or PPP) as part of a package of health care benefits to employees.

Local authorities

Local authorities provide community care services in their area, including care to help people live in their own home, as well as residential care homes.

Local initiatives for free food and drink

In an effort to ensure that children and young people get access to healthy nutritious food at school, some local authorities and schools use the powers that they have to provide free breakfasts, free lunches, free fruit or free milk to some children and young people for whom they are responsible.

Healthy programmes in schools

The Schools (Health Promotion and Nutrition) (Scotland) Act 2007, replaced the Hungry for Success programme. Its aim is to:
- place health promotion at the heart of school activities
- ensure that food and drink served in schools meets nutritional requirements as set out by Scottish ministers
- ensure local authorities promote the uptake and benefits of school meals and, in particular, free school meals
- reduce the stigma associated with free school meals by protecting the identity of those eligible for them.

Government policies and initiatives

The NHS, local government, local communities and the private sector are working together to tackle health inequalities by helping people to improve their health, especially in disadvantaged communities, and to ensure better, more local and faster access to health care.

Although the general health of people in Scotland is improving, the Scottish government has still to improve the country's poor health record. They have introduced a range of initiatives to encourage people to live healthier lives, reduce smoking and drug and alcohol abuse.

Aims to reduce smoking	The Scottish government has taken action to reduce smoking by introducing the following: ● the 2006 ban on smoking in public places ● the end of tobacco displays in shops ● the ban of tobacco sales from vending machines ● raising of the legal age for buying tobacco from sixteen to eighteen.
Alcohol Framework for Action	The aims of the Alcohol Framework for Action initiative are to reduce alcohol consumption and harm throughout Scotland through developing partnership work with the alcohol industry and by improving education and diversionary activities, such as sport, arts and culture.
Minimum pricing for alcohol	In June 2012 the Alcohol (Minimum Pricing, Scotland) Act was passed, which the Scottish government hopes will lead to the introduction of a 50p minimum price per unit of alcohol.
Drugs – Road to Recovery	The 'Road to Recovery' is the Scottish government's national drug strategy. The process of recovery helps a person who uses drugs to move towards a drug-free life.
Preventing drug misuse	The Road to Recovery also recognises that reducing future demand for drugs can only be achieved by addressing the root causes of problem drug use. The government is working to address poverty, deprivation and inequality; and to enhance children's experiences in their early years.
Drugs education	Drugs education in Scotland is firmly established within wider health and wellbeing education. 'Know the Score' offers information and advice and makes sure people are aware of the dangers of drugs.
Choices for Life	The 'Choices for Life' website gives information on issues such as drugs, alcohol and tobacco as well as Internet safety.
Equally Well	Equally Well is the Scottish government's framework aimed at reducing health inequalities within the Scottish population.
Achieving Our Potential	This scheme aims to tackle poverty and income inequality and has been followed up by a Child Poverty Strategy, which was published in March 2011.
The Early Years Framework	The Early Years Framework aims to ensure that all children are given the best possible start in life. It highlights the importance of all national and local agencies, the third sector and private sector working together to deliver improved outcomes for children.
Free prescriptions in Scotland	When the NHS was established by Labour in 1948, all prescriptions were free of charge. However, charging was introduced three years later. The SNP Administration abolished prescription charges in Scotland in April 2011, following the example of the Welsh assembly. Free prescriptions have not been introduced in England. The SNP public health minister said: 'Lifting the charge will save money in the long term, and will no longer put people off going to see their doctor. We believe that free prescriptions are a long-term investment in improving health.'

Table 6.4 Scottish government policies and initiatives aimed at encouraging people to live healthier lives

Figure 6.5 Measures have been taken to try to reduce smoking in Scotland

Questions and model answers

Describe question

Living in poverty has a huge effect on people and families in the UK.

Describe, **in detail**, the problems faced by people who experience poverty in the UK.

6 marks

Model answer

One problem can be living in a cold, damp house as the person will not be able to heat the house to a proper standard. This is called fuel poverty and with the massive increase in fuel costs, this is a growing problem. The person will be charged the highest prices possible as they will not be paying by direct debit. Families may have to decide whether to spend money on food or heating if they cannot afford both.

A second problem is that people living in poverty may experience poorer health than other people who don't live in poverty. Children living in poverty may have a poor diet of cheap food, as it is expensive to buy healthy food such as fruit and vegetables. Families living in poverty can also experience depression and low self-esteem. They can feel trapped and isolated.

Marker's comment

This is a very good answer because it is relevant and detailed. The candidate covers two factors. The first paragraph easily deserves three marks because it accurately identifies financial hardship. This is developed by referring to poor housing and fuel poverty, and further exemplification is provided by commenting on the financial choices families living in poverty may face.

The second paragraph would also get three marks because it accurately identifies ill health as an effect. This is developed by referring to poor diet, depression and low self-esteem.

Overall a very good and high quality answer deserving of full marks.

6 marks

Remember

Knowledge questions will have four, six or eight marks allocated and you will need to answer two questions — one describe question and one explain question.

Remember

In a describe question, up to three marks can be awarded for each description you make, depending on their quality, level of detail, relevance, accuracy and exemplification.

Hints & tips

In this describe question you could also have used any of the following factors that can cause people to experience poverty:

✓ low pay
✓ gender
✓ race
✓ education
✓ disability.

Explain question

Some people experience poorer health than others in the UK.

Explain, **in detail**, why some people experience poorer health than others in the UK. **6 marks**

Model answer

A person's lifestyle choices can lead to them experiencing poorer health than others in the UK. People who choose to smoke may experience poorer health than those who don't because it increases the risk of health conditions that can cause long-term damage and may be fatal. For example, smoking causes around 90% of lung cancers and is one of the biggest causes of death and illness in the UK. Also, drinking too much alcohol and taking drugs can lead to poor health. It has been shown that those who drink too much are more likely to have high blood pressure and liver disease than those who don't, and mental illness is higher among those who take drugs.

Where you live can lead to some people experiencing poorer health than others. Those in the most deprived areas not only die younger, but also spend more of their lives in poor health compared with those in the least deprived areas of the country. Therefore, poorer health is not just due to higher rates of smoking, drinking and drug-taking but is also linked to living in areas of deprivation and high unemployment. All this means that poor health is higher where deprivation and unemployment are higher. For example, differences in health are noticeable throughout Glasgow between the richest and poorest areas, such as less deprived Lenzie and more deprived Calton.

Marker's comment

This is a very good answer because it is relevant and detailed. The first paragraph would get four marks because it accurately identifies lifestyle choices (smoking, drinking and drugs) as leading to some people experiencing poorer health. This is developed with considerable and relevant detail. Exemplification is also included, with detailed statistics showing the interaction of various lifestyle choices. Furthermore, there is a good level of analysis throughout the paragraph.

The second paragraph would also receive four marks, if they were available, because it accurately identifies where you live as leading to some people experiencing poorer health. This is developed with considerable and relevant detail. Exemplification is also included through relevant comparison of Lenzie and Calton. Furthermore, there is a level of analysis between the two paragraphs with the comment:

'therefore, poorer health is not just due to higher rates of smoking, drinking and drug-taking but is also linked to living in areas of deprivation'.

Overall a very good and high quality answer deserving of full marks. As stated, the quality of both paragraphs would merit four marks each if needed, but six marks are all that is available.   **6 marks**

Chapter 7
Crime and the Law

What you should know

To be successful in this section, you should be able to:

★ **describe** and **explain** what is meant by crime and who is responsible for deciding what is criminal

★ **describe** and **explain** what the different types of crime are, including:
  ★ white collar and blue collar
  ★ theft and fraud
  ★ assault and rape
  ★ murder

★ **describe** and **explain** what the causes of crime are

★ **describe** and **explain** the impact of crime on local communities and individuals

★ **describe** and **explain** police efforts to tackle crime

★ **describe** and **explain** the laws regarding alcohol, drugs and road traffic offences, and how effective these laws are

★ **describe** and **explain** the criminal justice system in Scotland:
  ★ the Court of Session
  ★ the Justice of the Peace Courts and Sheriff Courts
  ★ the High Court of Justiciary

★ **describe** and **explain** what the differences in the above courts' procedures and the verdicts available to them are

★ **describe** and **explain** types of sentences:
  ★ custodial and non-custodial: evaluation of the advantages and disadvantages of different forms of sentencing

★ **describe** and **explain** the Scottish juvenile justice system:
  ★ Children's Hearings: their strengths and criticisms and their procedures and actions.

Who decides what is criminal?

In England and Wales the Crown Prosecution Service (CPS) is responsible for prosecuting criminal cases investigated by the police. In Scotland, the role of the CPS is taken by the Crown Office and Procurator Fiscal Service.

One of the key jobs of the CPS, Crown Office and Procurator Fiscal Service is deciding whether or not to charge a case. Even if the police have captured a suspect and gathered evidence, they can decide not to go ahead and take the suspect to court.

Key words

Crime: An action or omission that constitutes an offence and is punishable by law. A person who has broken a law or breached a rule is said to have committed a crime.

Types of crime

White-collar crime

People who work in offices and in sales roles are referred to as 'white-collar workers'. White-collar crime includes fraud, bribery and money laundering.

Blue-collar crime

People who work doing manual labour, for example a gardener or a carpenter, are referred to as 'blue-collar workers'. Blue-collar crime is more likely to involve physical force, either through breaking-and-entry or assault.

Theft and fraud

Theft is the generic term for all crimes in which a person intentionally and fraudulently takes the personal property of another without their permission or consent.

Fraud is an act of deception intended for personal gain or to cause a loss to another party. This can include someone deceiving or knowingly making false representation or failing to disclose information.

Damage to property

Damage to property can involve the injury to personal property through another's negligence or wilful destruction.

Traffic crime

The prosecution of traffic offences in the UK is considered vital to the enforcement and promotion of road safety and the protection of the public, with a wide variety of road traffic offences in place in order to punish those felt to be acting irresponsibly on the road.

Assault and rape

An assault is when a person directs an attack or physically harms another person, whether or not actual injury is inflicted. In Scotland, rape can only be committed by men, but the victim of rape can be a woman or a man. The mere threat of violence or even death is often used by rapists to force women to comply without a struggle. The law only requires that threats of physical violence are made.

Murder

Murder in Scotland is defined as an intent to kill or an act of wicked recklessness. According to a Professor of Scots Law at Aberdeen University, the typical murder in Scotland involves someone who goes out with a knife, has too much to drink and acts in a very violent way that presents very serious risk to other people.

Drug- and alcohol-related crime

With regard to offences committed 'under the influence' of drugs or alcohol, the implication is that they would not have happened or they would not have reached the level of seriousness that they actually did if the offender had been clean or sober. In the case of alcohol, it is generally accepted that it is a major causal link leading to crime, for example there is a proven relationship between alcohol and violent crime.

Drugs are related to crime in a variety of ways. Most directly, it is a crime to use, possess, manufacture or distribute drugs. Drugs are also related to crime through the effects they have on the user's behaviour and by leading to violence and other illegal activity in connection with drug trafficking.

What are the causes of crime?

Poverty

There is no direct link between poverty and crime; however, people who live in poverty may be more vulnerable to becoming involved in crime.

Crime offers a way for those living in poverty to obtain material goods that they could not otherwise afford. For many in poverty, the perceived rewards from crime can outweigh the risk of being caught, thus poverty can lead to increased crime rates.

Social exclusion

Higher levels of crime are associated with homelessness, poor health, and drug and alcohol misuse – all of which can lead to social exclusion. In fact, a criminal record can lead to social exclusion as it has an impact on the chances of getting a job and thereby pushes people further into crime and re-offending.

Lack of education

It has been shown that crime rates are inversely proportional to education levels. Young people who grow up in families that do not value education are more likely to live out on the streets, get involved in drug and alcohol abuse, join gangs and end up in prison.

Geographical location

A 'hot-spot' is an area in the UK that suffers from higher crime rates than other areas. Research shows that the highest rates of robberies and violent crime are often committed in poorer areas, which also have high levels of social problems.

Peer pressure

Peer pressure is when a person does something they normally would not do in order to fit into or impress a group. Many behave in ways the group approves of in order to feel they belong. This can often lead to involvement in drugs, alcohol, smoking, bullying or fighting, leading to criminal activity and trouble with the police.

Figure 7.1 Peer pressure can sometimes lead to anti-social behaviour or crime

Greed

Greed is the most common factor leading to corruption. Most of the recent corruption scandals have an element of greed associated with them. Greed is often a temptation for individuals to carry out a corrupt act, especially public officials who have control of large sums of money not belonging to them.

A crime rooted in greed

Carol Hawkins, a former aide to U2 star Adam Clayton, was jailed for seven years after embezzling almost 3 million euros, in what a judge labelled a crime 'rooted in greed'.

Hawkins splashed the stolen cash on 22 racehorses, exotic holidays, limousine services and in designer boutiques in New York, such as Roberto Cavalli. She bought a Volkswagen Golf for her son and paid for fashion and film courses for her children. 'These were crimes rooted in greed and nothing else,' said Judge McCartan.

Source: Adapted from the *Daily Record*, 6 July 2012

Activities

Create a spider diagram or concept map of the causes of crime.

What is the impact of crime?
On local communities and individuals

Crime in local communities can make daily life a real struggle for people across the UK. Anti-social behaviour (any activity that impacts on other people in a negative way) can ruin the quality of community life.

Anti-social behaviour can be targeted at individuals or specific groups of people or can be the result of general circumstances, such as youths on the street creating a feeling of intimidation. Noise disturbance caused by late-night fireworks is another example of anti-social behaviour.

Examples of anti-social behaviour include:
- nuisance neighbours
- intimidating groups taking over public places
- vandalism, graffiti, fly-tipping
- people taking and buying drugs on the street.

Victims

Many victims of crime go through a difficult adjustment period following the crime. Whether they have been physically hurt or had their house broken into, the stress and trauma felt is usually a reaction to the loss of safety and security brought about by the crime.

Victims of crime may feel fearful, angry, resentful or revengeful and easily agitated, anxious, easily startled and suspicious of everyone, violated and vulnerable.

The 2011 riots

In August 2011, riots that had begun in London spread to Manchester, Birmingham, Bristol and Liverpool. Five people died, 2,500 shops and businesses were damaged and over 2,000 participants were arrested and 1,400 sent to jail.

Figure 7.2 In 2011, riots spread across England

Activities

Use the Internet to investigate the causes of the Riots of 2011.

Efforts to tackle crime

The role of the police

In the UK, the main role of the police is to:

- maintain law and order and protect persons and property
- detect criminals and, in the course of interrogating suspects, play a part in the early stages of the judicial process.
- prevent crime
- control road traffic.

What are the laws regarding alcohol, drugs and road traffic offences?

Alcohol

Under fourteen: It is at the landlord's discretion whether children are allowed anywhere in a pub. They cannot, of course, buy or drink alcohol on the premises.

Sixteen or seventeen: In the UK sixteen and seventeen year olds are allowed to drink beer, wine or cider at a meal out with parents. In Scotland, they do not need to have an adult present to buy beer, wine or cider with a meal.

Under eighteen: It is against the law for anyone under eighteen to buy alcohol in a pub, supermarket or other licensed outlet in the UK. Furthermore, adults are not allowed to buy alcohol on behalf of under-eighteens in a licensed premise. The only exception is for sixteen and seventeen year olds (see above).

Police have powers to confiscate alcohol from under-eighteens drinking in public spaces (e.g. in the street or in parks).

Buying alcohol for those under eighteen

Police have the power to charge those over eighteen who knowingly buy alcohol for anyone under the legal drinking age ('buying by proxy').

Drugs

The laws controlling drug use in the UK are complicated. The Misuse of Drugs Act (MDA) regulates what are termed 'controlled drugs'. It divides drugs into three classes, Class A, Class B and Class C. Class A drugs are treated by the law as the most dangerous.

Offences under the Misuse of Drugs Act can include:
● possession of a controlled drug
● possession with intent to supply another person
● production, cultivation or manufacture of controlled drugs.

Certain controlled drugs, such as amphetamines, barbiturates, methadone, minor tranquillisers and occasionally heroin, can be obtained through a legitimate doctor's prescription. In such cases their possession is not illegal.

Road traffic offences

The prosecution of traffic offences in the UK is considered vital to the enforcement and promotion of road safety and the protection of the public, with a wide variety of road traffic offences in place in order to punish those felt to be acting irresponsibly on the road. However, many road traffic offences are minor in nature and for many offenders their prosecution will be their only experience of criminal law enforcement.

Category of offence	Offence
Accident offences	Failing to stop after an accident
	Failing to give particulars or to report an accident within 24 hours
Disqualified driver	Driving while disqualified
Careless driving	Driving without due care and attention
	Causing death through careless driving when unfit through drink/drugs/alcohol
Construction-and-use offences	Using a vehicle with defective brakes/tyre(s)
	Using a mobile phone while driving a motor vehicle
Reckless/dangerous driving	Dangerous driving
Drink/drugs	Driving or attempting to drive with alcohol level above limit
	Driving or attempting to drive when unfit through drugs
Insurance offences	Using a vehicle uninsured against third party risks
Licence offences	Driving otherwise than in accordance with a licence
Speed limits	Exceeding statutory speed limit on a public road
	Exceeding speed limit on a motorway

Table 7.1 Categories of driving offence

The Scottish criminal justice system

The Scottish system of courts

The Scottish Courts Service (SCS) runs the different courts that make up the Scottish legal system. The three main Scottish courts are:

- the Justice of the Peace Courts
- the Sheriff Court
- the High Court of Justiciary.

Court of Session

Scotland's supreme civil court is the Court of Session. The court sits as a court of first instance and a court of appeal in Parliament House in Edinburgh.

Justice of the Peace Courts

These criminal courts replaced District Courts. They deal with less serious criminal cases and road traffic cases. The judge is called a justice of the peace (sometimes shortened to JP). Normally the maximum fine this court can give is £2,500 and the longest prison sentence is 60 days.

Sheriff Court

The Sheriff Court involves 'summary' and 'solemn' trials. The judge is a qualified lawyer, known as a sheriff, who must have at least ten years' legal experience.

In summary criminal cases there is no jury and the sheriff decides whether the accused is guilty or not and then decides the sentence.

In solemn criminal cases, which are more serious cases, there is a sheriff and a jury. The jury decides whether the accused is guilty or not and the sheriff then decides the sentence.

- For summary criminal cases a sheriff can impose up to twelve months in prison and fines of up to £5,000.
- For solemn criminal cases a sheriff can sentence the accused for up to five years in prison and an unlimited fine.
- If the sheriff thinks that the crime deserves a higher sentence than they can pass they can refer the case to the High Court for sentence.

High Court of Justiciary

The High Court only deals with solemn proceedings involving a judge and a jury. The jury decides whether the accused is guilty or not and the judge then decides the sentence. The High Court deals with the most serious cases such as murder, rape and treason. Judges (not sheriffs or magistrates) sit in the High Court. In the High Court there is no limit on the length of sentence or amount of the fine that can be imposed, although the sentence for some crimes is limited by statute. The High Court also deals with all criminal appeal cases.

Verdicts

When the evidence of all the witnesses has been heard, the judge, sheriff or jury must reach their verdict or make their decision. In criminal cases, the possible verdicts are:

Not guilty

If the accused is found not guilty then the accused is free to go and cannot be prosecuted again on that charge.

Not proven

If the verdict is not proven then the accused is free to go. This verdict is unique to Scotland and is currently under review by the Scottish government. Labour MSP Michael McMahon has placed a Members' Bill before the Scottish parliament to scrap the not proven verdict. He argued that this verdict was preventing justice being done as it places a stain on the individual's character and leaves the victim and their family unhappy.

Guilty

If the accused is found guilty the judge will decide on the most appropriate sentence. There is a wide range of sentencing options depending on the nature of the crime and the background of the person who has been convicted.

Court sentencing powers

Court	Type of judge	Jury present	Sentencing powers
Justice of the Peace Court	Justice of the Peace	No	Maximum fine £2,500 Maximum prison sentence 60 days
Justice of the Peace Court – Stipendiary Magistrate	Stipendiary Magistrate (Glasgow only)	No	Maximum fine £5,000 Maximum prison sentence twelve months
Sheriff Court (summary)	Sheriff	No	Maximum fine £5,000 Maximum prison sentence twelve months
Sheriff Court (solemn)	Sheriff	Yes	Unlimited maximum fine Maximum prison sentence five years (or pass to High Court)
High Court	Judge	Yes	Unlimited maximum fine Unlimited maximum prison sentence

Table 7.2 Scottish courts and their sentencing powers

Sentences

A sentence is the punishment the courts decide should be given to someone who has been convicted of a crime. The aim of sentences is to:
- punish the offender
- reduce crime
- reform and rehabilitate offenders
- protect the public
- make the offender give something back to the people affected by the crime.

What is a Children's Reporter?

A Children's Reporter is a person who decides if a child needs to be referred to a Children's Hearing. They will get information about the child to help them make a decision. They might speak to a social worker, if the child has one, or to their teacher.

What is a referral?

A referral is information received by the Children's Reporter from anybody about a young person who may be in need of compulsory measures of supervision (legal intervention) to help them address their needs or behaviour. Most of the information about children and young people is received from the police, social work departments or schools.

What happens at the Children's Hearing?

Each hearing comprises three panel members. The panel members will listen to everyone and consider all the information. The hearing will then make a decision, and the panel members must give reasons for their decision.

What decisions can be made at a Hearing?

The panel members can decide:

- to discharge the case if formal, compulsory supervision measures are not required
- to continue the hearing at a later date if they need more information to help them make a decision about what is best
- to issue a warrant to keep the child in a safe place for up to three weeks until the next hearing, but only if this is necessary
- to make a supervision requirement if they consider that compulsory measures of supervision are needed to help the child.

What is a supervision requirement?

A supervision requirement can contain conditions stating where the child is to live and other conditions with which they must comply. The local authority is responsible for making sure that what is stated in the supervision requirement happens and that the child gets the help that they need. A supervision requirement has no set time limit, but should last only as long as is necessary and must be reviewed at least once a year when it can be continued, varied or stopped.

Source: Scottish Children's Reporter Administration

Questions and model answers

Describe question

The role of the police in Scotland is varied.

Describe, **in detail**, at least **two** roles of the police in Scotland.   **6 marks**

Model answer

Crime prevention is a role of the police in Scotland. This can be achieved by offering crime prevention advice to local people to make the areas they live in more safe and secure. For example, the police work with community organisations to prevent car theft by attending local meetings to offer advice on car protection and security.

Protecting the public is another role of the police in Scotland. This can involve stopping and searching individuals who the police feel are suspicious. For example, if they believe that a person may become involved in serious violence and that stopping and searching them could prevent that, or it is believed they are carrying a knife or dangerous weapon without good reason.

Marker's comment

This is a very good answer because it is relevant and detailed. The candidate covers two factors. The first paragraph would easily get three marks because it accurately identifies crime prevention as a role of the police. This is developed by detailed reference to crime prevention advice available to local people and detailed exemplification is provided by commenting on car theft.

The second paragraph would also easily get three marks because it accurately details public protection as a relevant role. This is further developed by referring to stopping and searching and detailed exemplification is provided by commenting on two reasons for stopping and searching people – preventing serious violence or knife carrying.

Overall a very good and high quality answer deserving of full marks.

6 marks

Remember

Knowledge questions will have four, six or eight marks allocated and you will need to answer two questions – one describe question and one explain question.

Remember

In a describe question, up to three marks can be awarded for each description you make, depending on their quality, level of detail, relevance, accuracy and exemplification.

Hints & tips

In answering this describe question you can pick up marks in a number of ways up to a maximum of six marks. You could also mention the following in your answer:

✓ maintain law and order
✓ detect crime
✓ be involved in the court system.

Arguments for immigration

- Immigrants bring their skills to the country, for example doctors, nurses and scientists.
- Immigrants bring different cultures to the country, offering diversity.
- Immigrants will often work for very low pay, for example in restaurants and hotels.
- Immigration often helps people from other countries to have a better life.

Arguments against immigration

- Drug dealers, terrorists and other criminals have an opportunity to enter the country through immigration.
- Poorer immigrants are able to use health care, education and welfare without paying taxes, putting a strain on government resources.
- National identity and language may become undermined through the influx of immigrants.
- Immigrants compete with Americans for low-paid jobs, especially those that require few skills to do.

Illegal immigration

After the 9/11 terrorist attacks, illegal immigration became an area of greater concern. The Secure Fence Act led to 700 miles of security fencing being erected along areas of the US/Mexico border that were known to be popular with drug traffickers and illegal immigrants. Around 6,000 National Guardsmen were also sent to the border to help with border control. Figures show that $1 billion (£632 million) has been spent to protect only 85 km (53 miles) of the border area.

Social factors

Health inequalities

Why are there health inequalities?

In the USA, citizens pay for health care through private medical insurance. There is no free health service as there is in the UK. Because of this, Americans who can afford to pay for the insurance are often healthier than those who cannot.

Many Americans do not have health insurance because:
- their employer does not provide cover
- they do not qualify for Medicare, which covers people over 65 years of age
- they do not qualify for Medicaid, the government-funded health care assistance for the poor.

Who experiences health inequalities?

There are around 7.3 million children in the United States who do not have health insurance, which amounts to 9.8% of all children in the country. The amount of children living in poverty who are also uninsured is 15.4%.

The groups most likely to be uninsured are the ethnic minorities. While just 13.9% of whites do not have insurance coverage, the same is true for 33% of Hispanics, 22% of blacks and 18% of Asians.

Government responses

The Affordable Care Act (ACA), passed by Congress and signed into law by President Obama in March 2010, gives people in the US greater health security. However, the Republicans are against this Act, claiming that it will mean higher health premiums for many Americans and that it takes away their right of choice. 'Obama Care', as the Republicans call ACA, came into force on 1 October 2013.

Before Affordable Care Act	After Affordable Care Act
People had to pay for health insurance.	Everyone in the US will be covered – from the poorest members in society to those who are wealthy.
Some companies gave employees health care.	Private health care will still be available.
Health insurance companies exploited people with health insurance.	The Act will rein in insurance companies.

Table 8.3 The effects of the Affordable Care Act, 2010

Education
Causes of inequality in education

- Location
- Poverty
- Language barriers
- Dropout rates.

Why are there inequalities in education?

In the USA, the state provides 50% of the money to operate schools and the rest comes from taxes on local property and sales. This means that prosperous areas can afford the best facilities, technology and teachers. Poorer areas often struggle to achieve the basic resources.

In **ghettos** and barrios (poor neighbourhoods) schooling is below the required standard because there are no funds to pay for teachers or resources. Home life is often difficult in these areas, and a lack of role models and help with learning at home helps to create a 'cycle of poverty'.

Students also lack funds to buy essential items for school and this can lead to problems with learning.

Government responses

The American Recovery and Reinvestment Act, 2009

The US government has stated that this Act has 'invested heavily in education both as a way to provide jobs and to lay the foundation for long-term prosperity'.

> **Key words**
>
> **Ghetto:** A run-down inner city area.

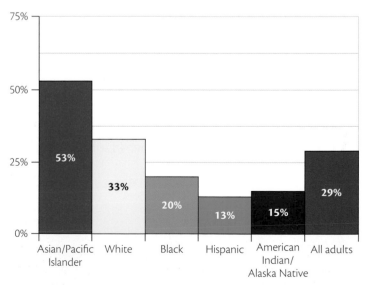

Figure 8.5 Percentage of adults with at least a bachelor's degree, by ethnicity, 2008

Housing

In America there are many different types of houses and neighbourhoods.

Ghettos vs suburbs

A ghetto is an area of an American city usually occupied by a minority group or groups, but especially black Americans. Ghettos often suffer from the problems shown in Figure 8.6 below. Residents of suburban areas, on the other hand, are often the same race, socioeconomic status and age. Suburban areas differ from ghettos in the ways shown in Figure 8.7.

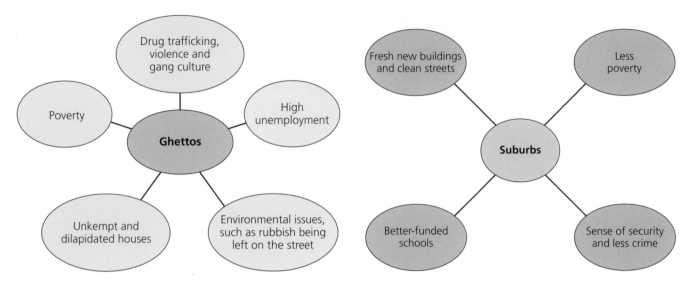

Figure 8.6 Disadvantages of living in ghettos

Figure 8.7 Advantages of living in the suburbs

Who experiences inequalities in housing?

Prior to the partial collapse of the banking system in 2007 followed by an economic recession, America had experienced a home ownership boom, especially among ethnic minorities. However, the collapse in the housing market has led to many low-paid families losing their homes as they cannot afford or are not willing to continue paying their mortgage on a house that is worth less than the mortgage. The home ownership rate for blacks fell from 48% in 2006 to 45% in 2011.

Government responses

Department of Housing and Urban Development (HUD)

The HUD is implementing a number of initiatives to provide quality, affordable homes for everyone.

Crime and law

In the USA most crimes take place in ghetto areas where the population is mostly made up from blacks and Hispanics. Because of this, ethnic minorities often appear to be discriminated against when being sentenced for crimes committed.

Who experiences inequalities?

More black people and Hispanic people are sent to prison than white people, and they are generally younger. There are:

- 1,319 black inmates on death row (41.9% of death row inmates).
- 390 Latino inmates on death row (12.4% of death row inmates).
- 1,358 white inmates on death row (43.2% of death row inmates).
- 79 'other' inmates on death row (2.5% of death row inmates).

Source: Bureau of Justice Statistics

Government responses

In response to continuing high levels of gun crime and high profile cases of mass shootings, the US government has tried to pass legislation to tighten up the regulation and ownership of guns, especially more dangerous 'assault' weapons. Changes that have been sought or secured include:

- Background checks are required for all gun sales.
- The background check system for gun sales is to be strengthened.
- There will be a new, stronger ban on assault weapons.
- The freeze on funding for gun violence research will be ended.

Economic factors

Unemployment

There is a wide range of reasons why there can be inequalities of unemployment between individuals, groups and regions. These can include:

- recession
- discrimination
- language barriers and illegal immigration
- lack of skills and qualifications.

Who experiences inequalities?

More blacks and Hispanics have been unemployed throughout the recession than other groups. Figures show that in 2010, 16% of black Americans and 12.5% of Hispanics were unemployed, against 8.7% for whites and 7.5% for Asians.

Government responses

The US government has responded with measures including:

American Recovery and Reinvestment Act (2009)	This Act has been responsible for about 3 million American jobs and has brought the economy back from the brink of another depression.
Dodd-Frank Wall Street Reform and Consumer Protection Act (2010)	This Act aims to put an end to bailouts and 'too big to fail' banking, and has enforced the strongest consumer protections in history.
Small Business Jobs Act (2010)	This Act provides tax breaks and better access to credit for millions of small businesses.

Table 8.4 US government responses to the economic recession

Wealth inequalities

Who experiences inequalities?

White Americans often earn more money than Americans of other races. There are a number of reasons for this:

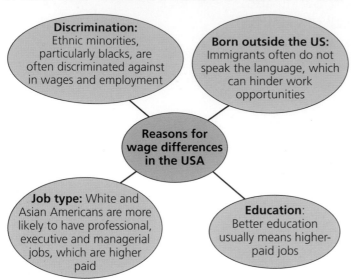

Ethnic group	Poverty rate (%)
Asian	12.3
White	9.8
Hispanic	24.4
Black	27.6

Source: US Census Bureau

Table 8.5 Poverty rates by ethnic group 2011

Figure 8.8 Some reasons for wage differences in the US

Government responses

The US government has introduced the American Recovery and Reinvestment Act to help vulnerable Americans have the means to afford food and have a home.

- The Act includes a $20 billion increase for the Supplemental Nutrition Assistance Program (SNAP), formerly known as Food Stamps, in an attempt to fight hunger.
- The Act provides increased income support as well as an extra payment to social security and supplemental security income beneficiaries and new resources for the Temporary Assistance for Needy Families (TANF) programme.

Rights and responsibilities

US citizens are entitled to a number of rights and privileges as they live in a democratic country, but they also have certain responsibilities regarding those rights.

Rights	Responsibilities
The right to free speech, a free press and freedom of religion	To respect the rights, beliefs and opinions of others
The right to vote	To register to use your vote
The right to bear arms	The right to own guns brings the responsibility to only use them in self-defence
The right to a fair and timely trial by a jury of your peers	To respect and obey federal, state and local laws

Table 8.6 Some rights and responsibilities of US citizens

Limitations on political rights

Some Americans claim that there are unfair limitations on their political rights.

Some of those who support the right to bear arms are unhappy with the restrictions on the types of guns they can buy.

Many black and Hispanic people are unhappy with recent changes to the Voting Rights Act, which will allow southern States to make changes which could make it harder for ethnic minorities to vote.

Questions and model answers

Describe question

In all G20 member countries, people can participate fully in the political process.

Describe, **in detail**, at least **two** ways that people in a G20 country that you have studied can participate in the political process. **6 marks**

Model answer

In America people have the opportunity to participate in the political process by joining an interest group like the National Rifle Association (NRA). This group puts pressure on the government to amend or introduce laws in support of its cause. Its members can participate in marches and demonstrations or organise petitions, letter campaigns, media campaigns and other forms of lobbying to gain public awareness and support.

American people can also participate in the political process by joining and supporting a political party, like the Democrats or Republicans. There are frequent elections in America, and the fact that the Presidential election campaign lasts for a year means that individual support is very important to the parties. A US citizen can participate by supporting a political party financially; this means giving the party money.

Marker's comment

In this answer, two factors are described. The first paragraph would get three marks because it accurately identifies joining an interest group as a relevant way to participate and also gives the example of the NRA putting pressure on the government to amend or introduce laws in support of its cause. Further exemplification is provided with reference to ways of gaining public awareness and support.

The second paragraph would also get three marks because it accurately details joining a political party as a relevant way to participate and gives the example of the Democrats or Republicans. This is further developed in detail by referring to elections, especially the Presidential election, and with further reference to the fact that parties can also be supported financially.

Overall a very good and high quality answer deserving of full marks
6 marks

Remember

Knowledge questions will have four, six or eight marks allocated and you will need to answer two questions — one describe question and one explain question.

Remember

In a describe question, up to three marks can be awarded for each description you make, depending on their quality, level of detail, relevance, accuracy and exemplification.

Explain question

There remain social and economic inequalities throughout all G20 countries today.

Explain, **in detail**, why social and economic inequalities remain in a G20 country you have studied. **6 marks**

Remember

For a six-mark answer you must cover at least two factors in depth. In an explain question, a maximum of four marks can be given for each detailed point you give, depending on their quality, level of detail, relevance, accuracy and exemplification. In your answer, it is also good to show the interaction of various factors.

Model answer

In America inequality exists in education because not all ethnic groups receive a full education. This is because dropout rates among the different ethnic groups vary widely. For example, a high dropout rate among Hispanics means they receive less education than whites, who have a low dropout rate. Since the majority of those eligible for free or reduced lunches are also Hispanic and a minority are white it seems that educational dropout rates could be linked to poverty. This is also seen later in life since education can affect wages because it can lead to a higher paid job.

Inequality also exists because not all ethnic groups earn the same wages. The types of jobs done by different ethnic groups vary. For example, white and Asian Americans tend to have the highest incomes and are more likely to have professional, executive and managerial occupations than blacks, Hispanics or American Indians, who have the lowest incomes. This could be due to discrimination especially against blacks or even difficulties for immigrants in speaking English that prevents them getting a job.

Marker's comment

In this answer the first paragraph would get three marks because it accurately identifies education as a reason why social and economic inequalities remain. This is developed in detail with reference to dropout rates and exemplified with links to race.

The second paragraph would also get three marks because it accurately identifies wages and job types as reasons why social and economic inequalities remain. This is developed and exemplified with relevant detail by mentioning incomes and professions and linking them to race.

So, overall a very good and high quality answer deserving of full marks. **6 marks**

Hints & tips

✓ Always structure your answers in paragraphs. Avoid list-type answers or bullet points.

✓ Make sure you take account of how many marks a question is worth. You should base the length of your answers on the time you should allocate to four mark, six mark or eight mark questions.

Chapter 9

World Powers: The Republic of South Africa

What you should know

To be successful in this section, you should:

★ **know** why South Africa is a regional superpower and why it is important to us here in Scotland
★ **know** the main features of its political structure, including:
  ★ its type of government
  ★ its main institutions of government
  ★ how people can participate
★ **understand** its socioeconomic issues, such as:
  ★ employment
  ★ wealth and health inequalities
  ★ education
  ★ housing
  ★ crime and law
★ **understand** the nature and extent of social and economic inequalities and the form and effectiveness of government responses
★ **describe and explain** the extent to which South Africa could be considered to be democratic
★ **know** the rights and responsibilities of individuals within South Africa.

Key words

Constitutional Court: The highest court of the land and guardian of the constitution.

Black Transformation: Government legislation to ensure that senior posts in the public and private sector reflect the racial composition of South Africa.

South Africa as a regional superpower

South Africa is the only country in sub-Saharan Africa to be a member of the G20 and the only country from Africa to host the football World Cup finals, which took place in 2010. It is a regional superpower and has by far the strongest economy in central and southern Africa.

Until 1994, South Africa was ruled by the minority white population, who denied the black majority their political, social and economic rights. This **apartheid** (separate development) system ended when Nelson

World Powers: The People's Republic of China

What you should know

To be successful in this section, you should be able to:
- ★ **describe** and **explain** political issues in China, such as:
  - ★ its type of government
  - ★ its main institutions of government
  - ★ how people can participate
- ★ **describe** and **explain** the extent to which China could be considered to be democratic
- ★ **understand** socioeconomic issues and government reactions and responses, including:
  - ★ population issues (overpopulation and internal migration)
  - ★ wealth and health inequalities
  - ★ education
  - ★ housing
  - ★ crime and law
- ★ **describe** and **explain** the rights and responsibilities of individuals within China.

Political issues

Communist Party of China

The political **ideology** of China is communism and this explains the complete control that the Communist Party of China (CPC) has over the political and social lives of the citizens of China. The party rules on behalf of the Chinese people and only at the local level do Chinese citizens directly elect their representatives.

In every village there is a local party official who keeps an eye on everything that is going on. Being a party member can mean significant privileges, which is why membership is continuing to rise.

Politburo

The Politburo does all the political decision-making in China.

Key words

Ideology: A set of political beliefs which guide the government of a country.

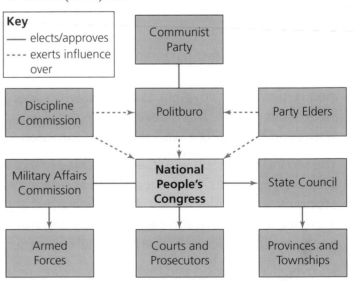

Source: BBC

Figure 10.1 The structure of government in China

The National People's Congress

The National People's Congress (NPC) is the legislative branch, or parliament, of China's government.

The Discipline Commission

The Discipline Commission investigates and deals with corruption among party cadres.

The Central Military Affairs Commission

The CMAC controls the People's Liberation Army (PLA) and the paramilitary People's Armed Police.

The Armed Forces

The People's Liberation Army (PLA) is seen as the defender of the CPC.

The State Council

China's State Council is responsible for implementing party policy from national to local level.

Provinces and townships

China has 22 provinces, five 'autonomous' regions, four municipalities and two special administrative regions. Decisions are made in the provinces and are then implemented downwards to the counties and into the cities and towns at the local level.

Special Administrative Regions (SARs)

Hong Kong and Macao were established as Special Administrative Regions of China and are based on the 'one country, two systems' concept, where their capitalist system and China's socialist system, and the different ideologies of both, work together.

Participation in the political process

Chinese citizens can be involved in the political process in many ways.

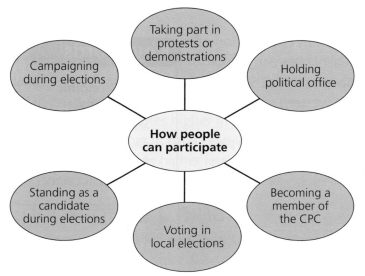

Figure 10.2 Ways that Chinese people can participate in the political process

Figure 10.3 China's new leader-President Xi Jinping and Premier Li Keqiang

Explain question

There remain social and economic inequalities throughout all G20 countries today.

Explain, **in detail**, why social and economic inequalities remain in a G20 country you have studied.

6 marks

Model answer

In China inequality exists in education because not all children receive a full education. All children are entitled to nine years of free education up to age fifteen. While most families in cities can afford to pay education fees after age fifteen, in rural parts of China many students have to stop their education then because of the cost. According to the World Bank this affects three main groups of people – the rural poor, girls and migrants.

In China inequality exists in wages and working conditions because not all workers are treated the same. For example, the average monthly income for migrant workers in 2013 was well below the national urban average. As migrant workers do not have the same hukou status as locals, many employers do not provide them with the same benefits as local workers. This may be because they are subject to institutional discrimination, including low wages and harsh working conditions.

Marker's comments

In this answer the first paragraph would get three marks because in the first sentence it accurately identifies education as a reason why social and economic inequalities remain. This is developed in detail with reference to entitlement and uptake with interaction provided by linking it to cost. Further exemplification is provided by mentioning the groups affected.

The second paragraph would also get three marks because it accurately identifies wages and working conditions as reasons why social and economic inequalities remain. This is developed and exemplified with relevant detail by mentioning incomes and worker status and the connection between them.

So, overall a very good and high quality answer deserving of full marks.

6 marks

Remember

In an explain question, up to four marks can be awarded for each explanation you give, depending on their quality, level of detail, relevance, accuracy and exemplification. It is also good practice to show the interaction of a variety of factors in your answers. At least two explanations are required in order to achieve full marks.

Chapter 11
World Issues: Development Issues in Africa

What you should know

To be successful in this section, you should:

★ **know** the economic, social and political factors affecting development
★ **know** the consequences of the lack of development on the African people
★ **know** in what ways human rights in Africa are compromised
★ **understand** how developed nations are working to help Africa
★ **understand** how international organisations, such as the following, are working to help Africa:
    ★ African Union
    ★ UN specialised agencies and NGOs.

Remember

Relevant examples from the countries of Africa are important when answering exam questions. You will find useful examples throughout this revision text.

Developed and developing countries

	Developed countries	Developing countries
Key terms	Rich North First World	Poor South Third World
Characteristics	● high standard of living ● good health services ● high literacy levels ● low infant mortality rates ● economies based on industry, trade and new technologies ● democratic.	● low standard of living ● poor health care services ● low literacy levels (high illiteracy) ● high infant mortality rates ● economies based on agriculture and there is a lack of modern technology and labour skills ● corrupt governments.
Countries	UK, USA, France, Germany, Australia, Japan and Canada.	Nigeria, Sudan, Angola, DR Congo, Chad and Mali.

Table 11.1 Developed and developing nations

Background

In total, around 1 billion people live in the continent of Africa, which is made up from 54 independent countries.

Although Africa is rich in natural resources, such as oil, diamonds, gold, iron, timber and tropical fruits, eighteen of the twenty poorest countries in the world are in sub-Saharan Africa and around 70% of Africa's population lives on less than $2 a day. More than 40% of the population is under fifteen years of age in many African countries, particularly those below the Sahara desert.

Malaria is a disease transmitted by mosquitoes. It is one of the leading causes of death and disease in the developing world but it is preventable and treatable. Untreated malaria kills more than 1 million people each year, many of them in sub-Saharan Africa. Children under five are most at risk with 75% of deaths occurring in that age group.

Education

School enrolment in African countries is the lowest in the world, with 33 million children not attending primary school. Pupils who do attend school often do not have basic facilities or resources and can be in classes of between 40 and 70 pupils.

Other factors
Climate change

In parts of Kenya it has become 3.5°C hotter over the past twenty years. Changes in the weather make working the land and growing crops more difficult for farmers. This is causing unemployment, loss of earnings and **famine**.

Natural disasters

Climate change is also a factor in droughts and flooding in Africa, which are becoming increasingly common. These have a major effect on people's lives as they affect food and water supplies as well as general everyday living. The financial cost of recovering from a natural disaster can exceed $1 billion and places enormous pressure on government resources.

What are the consequences of underdevelopment?

Lack of development has caused serious problems for the people of Africa, such as malnutrition, war and disease. This is an international issue that needs to be tackled immediately.

Lack of social services

Debt and trade issues mean that many African countries lack the type of social services we expect in Scotland. Schools often lack basic amenities such as electricity and running water. Hospitals are underfunded and under-resourced with too few doctors and nurses; many people living in rural areas have no educational or health facilities at all. Angola's debt highlights the problem – Angola spends 6.8% of its GDP on loan repayments and only 1.5% on health spending.

The impact of armed conflict

The civil war in Sudan has claimed the lives of 1.5 million people. In Darfur in western Sudan the conflict is ongoing; 2 million people have been displaced and more than 200,000 killed. Pro-government forces have

Key words

Famine: An extreme shortage of food.

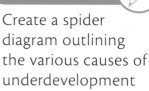

Activities

Create a spider diagram outlining the various causes of underdevelopment in Africa.

been accused of carrying out targeted **genocide** against the non-Arab people of Darfur. Death rates of infants and under-fives are very high in Sudan with one in eight children not living to age five. The conflict prevents many people from getting safe drinking water and sanitation facilities. Many people who have had to leave their homes are now refugees in Chad, a neighbouring country.

Child soldiers

Children are being forced to participate in wars, fighting as **child soldiers**, in some African countries. Around 60% of the 250,000 child soldiers in the world are thought to be in Africa. Child soldiers are currently being used in armed conflicts in Central African Republic, Chad, DR Congo, Mali, Somalia and Sudan.

Many child soldiers suffer psychological effects for a long time after the fighting has ended. They are often badly affected by things they have done and seen and become desensitised to violence. Most child soldiers will have missed out on school and without an education they have very few future prospects.

Figure 11.3 Child soldiers in Africa

Disease and HIV/AIDS

Diseases such as malaria and the AIDS epidemic have had an enormous effect on social and economic development in Africa. They place a huge strain on medical services and hospitals are struggling to cope with the number of AIDS patients. Around one-third of the population of Botswana has the AIDS virus, which prevents sufferers from working and contributing to the economy, and severely lowers life expectancy.

Famine and malnutrition

Famine can be the result of natural disaster, such as drought which causes low food production, or armed conflict where access to food is severely restricted. Around 275 million Africans are thought to go hungry every day and it is estimated that one-third of people living in sub-Saharan Africa are undernourished. Children are often victims of **malnutrition**. Poor nutrition is a major contributor to around 50% of child deaths in Africa. Malnutrition makes diseases such as measles and malaria much worse.

Lack of human rights

Everyone is entitled to human rights. After the end of the Second World War, the United Nations made a list of basic rights that all humans should have. These were set out in the 1948 Universal Declaration of Human Rights. Some of these rights are as follows:

Key words

Genocide: The attempt to wipe out a racial group.

Malnutrition: A general term that indicates a lack of some or all nutritional elements necessary for human health.

UN Universal Declaration of Human Rights

The right to life, liberty and security.

The right to take part in politics.

The right to freedom of speech.

The right to an education.

A lot of Africans will not be able to enjoy some of these human rights because of what is happening in their country. In every African country there is likely to be at least one factor to prevent citizens from accessing their full human rights as set out by the UN.

Right	How it is compromised
The right to life, liberty and security	This right will be compromised in an African country that is locked in conflict. The threat of violence and rape can be a daily worry for those in countries such as Sudan and Mali.
The right to take part in politics	Not every country in Africa has a democratic political system. In countries where there is a long established dictatorship, taking part in a fair political process will rarely happen.

Table 11.2 How human rights are compromised in Africa

Children's rights

The United Nations Convention on the Rights of the Child (CRC) gives all children the same rights based on what a child needs to survive, grow, participate and fulfil their potential. These rights apply equally to every child, regardless of where they are from or who they are. However, the chance of a child enjoying any or all of these rights is severely reduced if they are from Africa.

Activities

Create a spider diagram outlining the various consequences of underdevelopment in Africa.

What efforts are being made to help Africa?

Individual countries, non-governmental organisations (NGOs) and international organisations are all working to improve the situation in Africa and to address the many issues the continent faces.

Developed nations

Developed nations give aid, which can help poorer countries to overcome the challenges they face. Aid can be given in different forms, from humanitarian emergency assistance for disasters such as droughts or earthquakes, to longer term development aid. It is important that the aid goes towards targeting the specific problems of that nation. There are three main types of aid as outlined in Table 11.3.

Type of aid	Source of aid	Description
Bilateral	From one government to another.	Developed countries will target specific countries that require aid. Britain's bilateral aid is organised by the Department for International Development (DFID).
Multilateral	Aid given by international organisations.	Multilateral aid is given by international organisations such as the European Union (EU) and the United Nations (UN).
Voluntary aid	Aid given by NGOs or charities.	Many NGOs, such as Oxfam, fund specialised projects in developing countries, such as building schools or installing water pumps.

Table 11.3 The different types of aid

Tied aid

Tied aid is bilateral aid that has conditions attached whereby the country receiving the aid must use it to buy services and goods from the donor country. The donor county also benefits in this type of situation.

UK aid to African countries

The UK Department for International Development (DFID) promotes development in the developing world, particularly in countries where there is extreme poverty.

DFID works alongside charities, businesses and international organisations such as the World Bank and the UN to achieve the Millennium Development Goals (MDGs) (see page 111).

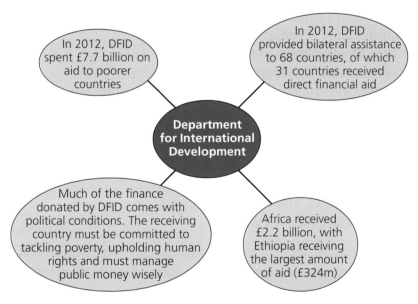

Figure 11.4 Some of the work of DFID

The African Union (AU)

The AU promotes democracy and human rights in Africa by stimulating the economy. It was founded in 2002 to help bring peace to Africa by reducing conflict there. During times of conflict the AU will provide a military presence to protect the citizens of the countries involved. The AU worked with the Somali government in 2013 to fight the terrorist group al-Shabaab, which tried to take over the country.

Chapter 12

World Issues: International Terrorism

What you should know

To be successful in this section, you should:

★ **know** what the causes of terrorism are
★ **recall** the events of major terrorist attacks
★ **understand** how terrorism has changed the world
★ **understand** links between human rights and terrorism
★ **know** how the United Kingdom has responded to terrorism
★ **know** how the international community has responded to terrorism.

The causes of terrorism

Terrorist attacks aim to achieve nationalist, political or religious goals. However, the causes of terrorism may overlap and a terrorist group may be active due to religious hatred and nationalist or political goals.

Nationalism

Scotland has been part of the United Kingdom since 1707, but some Scots think it is time that Scotland became a separate country in its own right. These people are called nationalists.

Throughout the world other people want independence for their own countries or regions, but feel this cannot be achieved peacefully so turn to violence and terrorism to achieve their goals. These people are sometimes called separatists.

Politics

Some countries are run by corrupt governments or **dictatorships**. In such countries rebels often take part in terrorist activities to try to force social and political change. However, these rebel groups are often supported by a large portion of the population, who would welcome the proposed changes. The civil war in Syria is an example of such a situation.

Religion

Religion has been associated with terrorism for centuries, with Northern Ireland being a recent example. People who commit terrorist attacks in the name of their religion are called religious extremists. Islamic religious extremists were behind the 9/11 attacks in the USA, and many other terrorist attacks during the last twenty years. They believe the West should not get involved in problems in the Middle East, or in wars such as Iraq and Afghanistan. Islamic extremists believe they are acting on behalf of God by waging a jihad (holy war) against the West by carrying out terrorist attacks and atrocities, for which they believe they will become martyrs and be rewarded in the afterlife.

Key words

Nationalism: Nationalists believe that independence should be sought due to a common culture, heritage and language.

Dictatorship: A form of government in which a person or a small group rules with almost unlimited power.

Radicalisation: A process where a person or group increasingly adopts extreme political, social or religious views or ideas.

Other factors

Poverty and discrimination can also be fertile ground for terrorists. For example, in Somalia in Africa most of the current generation of Somalis have grown up in conditions of conflict, insecurity of livelihood and deprivation. This has tended to make many of them vulnerable to the arguments and promises of militant group al-Shabaab.

Activities

Create a spider diagram outlining the various causes of terrorism.

The impact of terrorism

'International terrorism' is the phrase now used to describe the many terror attacks that have occurred worldwide since 9/11. It brings home the idea that terrorism is now worldwide, not confined to countries in conflict.

9/11

The most infamous terror attack was made by the terrorist group al-Qaeda on the United States of America.

On 11 September 2001, four American Airlines passenger planes were hijacked by nineteen al-Qaeda terrorists. Two of the planes were crashed by the terrorists into the Twin Towers of the World Trade Center in New York City, and a third plane destroyed part of the Pentagon (the US military headquarters). Following a struggle between hijackers and passengers, the fourth plane crashed in the countryside near Pittsburgh. Its original destination was Washington DC, where the White House is. Almost 3,000 people died in these attacks.

Who are al-Qaeda?

Osama bin Laden founded al-Qaeda in the late 1980s. The group is intensely opposed to the United States and other Western, democratic nations. Although based mainly in Afghanistan, al-Qaeda has followers working in many countries worldwide. It is almost impossible to fight al-Qaeda in a traditional war because of the way in which the group is set up, and therefore it is very difficult to defeat or stop them.

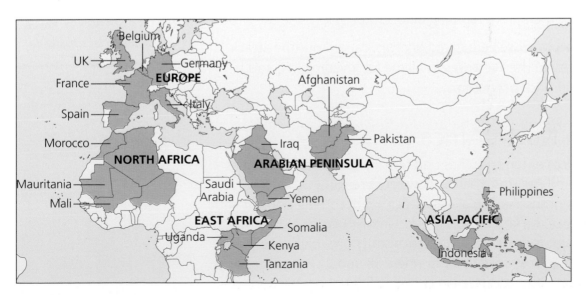

Figure 12.1 The main countries in which al-Qaeda operates

Al-Qaeda's leader Osama bin Laden was discovered in Pakistan and assassinated by US Special Forces in 2011.

Al-Qaeda: a history of terrorist attacks

As well as 9/11, al-Qaeda has been linked to other terrorist attacks:

1993: World Trade Center bombing

1998: US Embassy bombing in Kenya and Tanzania

2002: Bali bombing

2004: Madrid bombings

2005: London bombings

2008: Danish Embassy bombing in Pakistan

2013: Westgate shopping mall attack in Kenya

London bombings

In July 2005, 52 people were killed and more than 770 injured when four terrorists detonated three bombs on the London Underground and one on a London bus. The terrorists were young men between the ages of 18 and 30. They appear to have been motivated by the UK's Middle Eastern foreign policy and a hatred of the West. The men are also believed to have been radicalised through the Internet by logging on to extremist websites and learning how to make bombs.

Terror attack at Glasgow Airport

Glasgow Airport was attacked on 30 June 2007 when two terrorists crashed a vehicle packed with gas canisters in the main doors of the terminal building. The terminal building and the vehicle caught fire but the canisters did not explode. The terrorists were caught by police and civilians to prevent them from harming innocent people inside the airport.

The terrorists, who were well-educated doctors, carried out the attack because they believed the West was to blame for invading Iraq and for the deaths of thousands of Muslims.

Trouble in North Africa

Although the threat of terrorism has traditionally come from countries like Afghanistan and Pakistan, there is now more terrorist activity in North Africa. Countries like Somalia and Mali are becoming popular with terrorists because of the lack of policing and infrastructure. North Africa has become a major focus for counter-terrorism efforts, particularly since the Algerian hostage crisis in early 2013 where 38 people were killed, and the Westgate shopping mall attack in Kenya, in September 2013, in which at least 72 people died.

> ### Hints & tips ★
>
> *When answering an exam question on the consequences of an international issue like terrorism it is important that you know some of the major terrorist attacks to use as examples.*

Has the world changed since 9/11?

Since 9/11 the world has changed dramatically. The USA and Britain are at war in the Middle East, supporting the **war on terror**. Western governments have increased security measures to reduce the threat to their countries. The Western population now lives with the risk of terrorism in their everyday lives.

Security has been increased at UK airports. Before 9/11 air passengers were able to take bottled water and items such as scissors in their hand luggage but this is now forbidden. There are also stricter security systems to pass through, for example London Heathrow Airport uses a biometrics system to scan passengers' eyes and check them against a database. There are also more armed police in the departure areas.

Key words

War on terror: An international military campaign to eliminate al-Qaeda and other terrorist organisations.

How does terrorism impact the human rights of civilians around the world?

Human rights are universal rights to which everyone is entitled. In 1948, after the Second World War, the United Nations drew up a list of basic rights that all humans should have. These rights can be found in the 1948 Universal Declaration of Human Rights. (See page 108 for a list of some of these universal rights.)

Terrorism hopes to destroy human rights, destabilise governments and spread fear throughout countries. It aims to reduce people's feelings of security and prevent them from enjoying some human rights, including the rights to life and liberty. Everyone should be entitled to live their life peacefully without the threat or fear from terrorist crimes such as bombings, murder, intimidation or kidnapping.

Human rights in Afghanistan

Before 2001, Afghanistan was ruled by the **Taliban**, who ran the country using an extreme form of Islam called sharia law. The citizens of Afghanistan, especially women, had very few human rights. Under this system women had to be covered from head to toe and were not allowed to work, play sports or wear make-up.

The USA led an invasion into Afghanistan in 2001 and since then progress has been made on human rights. The country is now controlled by a democratic government. But human rights in Afghanistan are still poor compared to Scotland. The Taliban is still present in many areas of the country and works against the decisions of the government.

Figure 12.2 Malala Yousafzai, a Pakistani schoolgirl who challenged the Taliban ban on female education, was shot in the head by gunmen who stopped her school bus and asked for her by name. Taliban militants specifically targeted Malala for her work in encouraging women's education and rights. Malala survived her attack and is recovering after being flown to the UK for specialised medical treatment. In 2013 she addressed the UN General Assembly and was nominated for the Nobel Peace Prize.

How has the UK responded to international terrorism?

The war on terror began in 2001 with the invasion of Afghanistan in search of Osama bin Laden, leader of al-Qaeda. The war on terror continues today under the command of Barack Obama, who calls it the Overseas Contingency Operation. Many armed forces from the USA and the UK are still present in Afghanistan and continue to search out and fight terrorist organisations. It was announced in 2012 that the UK would reduce the number of troops in Afghanistan by 3,800 by the end of 2013 as the country is becoming more stable.

Counter terrorism

The UK government's counter-terrorism strategy is called 'CONTEST' and has four main aims:

1 The government will work to *pursue* terrorists and disrupt their work.
2 They will *prevent* terrorism by countering the various factors that cause people to become terrorists.
3 The government will work to *protect* the public through increased vigilance and security.
4 Lastly, they will *prepare for* and minimise the potential harm caused by terrorist attacks if they do occur.

The Scottish government works within this strategy and operates its own special counter-terrorism unit called the 'Scottish Preventing Violent Extremism Unit'.

The role of the police

The threat of terrorism has changed the role of police in our society. Police forces now train officers specifically in counter-terrorism. Police also track 'online terrorist activity', known as cyber-terrorism, and are able to watch over the Internet for people using cyberspace to promote, glorify or help carry out acts of terrorism and violent extremism.

How has the international community responded to terrorism?

The USA

Since 9/11, America has led the fight against international terrorism. However, many argue that the USA is actually increasing terrorist activity through its actions, for example in Afghanistan, as opposed to stopping it.

US drone attacks

The US has increasingly used 'unmanned aerial vehicles', known commonly as drones, to target terrorists living in remote areas in countries such as Pakistan and Afghanistan. Drones have multiple uses such as gathering intelligence through surveillance, listening to mobile phone conversations and actively attacking suspected terrorists. However, the use of drones has been criticised as drones have killed hundreds of innocent people in the hunt for suspected terrorists. It is this sort of tactic employed by the USA that is said to fuel terrorism.

The death of Osama bin Laden

In May 2011, US special forces found and killed Osama bin Laden, leader of al-Qaeda and the mastermind behind the 9/11 terrorist attacks, who had been living in Pakistan. This was a major breakthrough for the USA and the international community in the fight against terrorism. Bin Laden was not only the head of al-Qaeda but he was seen by extremists around the world as the leader in the fight against the West.

Figure 12.3 Osama bin Laden

The response of international organisations to terrorism

Two important international organisations that help to prevent and stop terrorist attacks on their members are the United Nations (UN) and the North Atlantic Treaty Organization (NATO).

The United Nations

Countries joining the UN agree to work together to maintain peace and security in the world. Through the UN the international community has agreed on a global strategy to combat terrorism.

Explain question

Explain, **in detail**, the causes of an international issue or problem you have studied.   **8 marks**

Model answer

There are various causes of terrorism. Firstly, a group may resort to terrorist acts to try and achieve a nationalist goal. This means they believe their region or country should have independence from another country. It may also include two countries fighting over an area of land, such as is the case in the dispute between Palestine and Israel.

Another reason a group may resort to terrorism is due to religious extremism. Muslim extremists strongly disagree with the US military presence in the Middle East (Holy Land) and the Western way of life in general. Al-Qaeda has carried out terrorist attacks against Western countries for this reason, none more infamous than 9/11.

Political reasons may cause a group to resort to terrorist activities. In poorer developing countries governments may be corrupt dictatorships and treat citizens badly. In turn, people may resort to violence against government forces to try and bring about social and political change within their country. An example of this situation is currently happening in Syria.

Other reasons can also be considered causes of terrorism. If a particular group within a country faces discrimination from the majority of people they may resort to terrorism in retaliation. Similarly, poverty can be regarded as a cause of terrorism. In Somalia most of the current generation of Somalis have grown up in conditions of conflict and deprivation. This has tended to make many of them vulnerable to the arguments and promises of terrorist group al-Shabaab.

Marker's comment

This is an eight mark question so requires a response of good length and depth. The answer clearly outlines the main causes of terrorism and for each gives relevant up-to-date examples. In each paragraph there is analysis and a clear explanation of each cause of terrorism – like the question asks. The point, explain, example structure is apparent to see, which is a useful way to ensure you create paragraphs that will pick up good marks. This answer would easily achieve 8/8.

                                                                8 marks

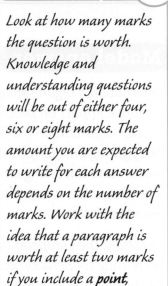

Hints & tips

Look at how many marks the question is worth. Knowledge and understanding questions will be out of either four, six or eight marks. The amount you are expected to write for each answer depends on the number of marks. Work with the idea that a paragraph is worth at least two marks if you include a **point**, **explanation** and **example** (P.E.E.).

Part Five: Source-based questions

There are three types of skills questions and you will have practised these in your classwork and passed them as part of your unit assessment. The three source-based skills are as follows:

- Using sources of information to identify and explain the selective use of facts. This will have been assessed in your **Democracy in Scotland and the UK** unit.
- Using sources of information to make and justify a decision. This will have been assessed in your **Social Issues in the UK** unit.
- Using sources of information to draw and support conclusions. This will have been assessed in your **International Issues** unit.

Remember

In your course exam the source-based questions can appear in any of the three units, so selective use of facts could be a question in the International Issues section of the exam.

Questions that assess the evaluation of sources will be allocated either eight or ten marks.

To achieve full marks, you must refer to all sources in your answer. A maximum of **four** marks will be awarded if just one source is used and a maximum of **six marks** if only two sources are used.

You can gain a maximum of **three** marks for each well-developed point you make.

Remember

Remember that when answering this question the marker is looking for you to be able to evaluate a limited range of sources, **detecting** and **explaining** instances of selectivity in the use of facts, giving developed **arguments**.

☞ Detecting — you must identify evidence from the sources that does not support the viewpoint (selective in use of facts). You should also be identifying evidence from the sources that does support the viewpoint (not selective in use of facts).

☞ Explaining — you should then use this evidence in your answer to explain why it is being selective/not selective. You should quote from the viewpoint and highlight which source the evidence is from.

☞ Argument — you should try to include some evaluative language to enhance your arguments, for example, in commenting on a figure of 10%, you could say that 'only one in ten...' or when looking at a figure of over 50% you could say 'the majority of people....'

Democracy in Scotland

The following shows an example of how to use sources of information to identify and explain the selective use of facts.

Skills question

Study sources one, two and three below, then attempt the question that follows.

Source One

The fourth Scottish parliament election took place in May 2011. The election was held using a proportional representation system called the Additional Member System. This system aims to give a fairer and more proportional result and is designed to ensure that usually no one party gains an overall majority, to encourage consensus. This was the case in 1999 and 2003 where the vote returned a Labour/Lib Dem Coalition and in 2007 where the SNP had a minority government. However, in 2011 the SNP successfully gained majority control of the parliament.

⇨

Voters were given two ballot papers, giving voters in Scotland more choice: one used to elect each of 73 constituency members and the second to elect seven members from each of eight electoral regions. This also ensures greater proportionality than the UK general election. As the system is more proportional than the First Past The Post system that is used in the UK general election, it is intended to reduce voter apathy and improve participation.

Also, since its inception the Scottish parliament elections have always returned representation for smaller parties, for example in 2003 there were seventeen MSPs outside the main political parties. It was not until the 2010 general election that the Green Party gained its first MP in the UK parliament. Following the creation of a majority SNP Government there will be an independence referendum in 2014 in which the people of Scotland will decide on the country's place within the United Kingdom.

Source Two

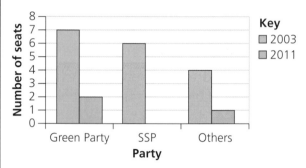

Comparison of the 2003 and 2011 Scottish parliament election results for minority parties

Source Three

| Party | 2010 UK general election | | 2011 Scottish parliament election | |
	Votes %	Seats %	Votes %	Seats %
Conservative	36.1	47.2	12.4	11.6
Labour	29.0	39.7	26.3	28.7
Liberal Democrat	23.0	8.7	5.2	3.9
SNP	1.7	0.009	44.0	53.5

Comparison of the 2010 UK general election and the 2011 Scottish parliament elections

Using sources one, two and three, explain why David Watt is **selective in his use of facts**.

'The 2011 Scottish parliament election showed that the Additional Member System is fit for purpose as it encourages participation and is more representative.'

David Watt

In your answer you must:

- give evidence from the sources that supports David Watt's view.
- give evidence from the sources that opposes David Watt's view.

Your answer must be based on all three sources. **8 marks**

One way in which David Watt is being selective in the use of facts is when he says 'The 2011 Scottish parliament election showed that the Additional Member System is fit for purpose as it encourages participation and is more representative'. This is because source two states that under AMS the SNP gained a majority share of the seats even though AMS 'is designed to ensure that usually no one party gains an overall majority, to encourage consensus'. This is backed up by source three, which shows that the SNP gained a massive 53.5% share of the seats. This is not representative as they gained less than half of the percentage share of votes – 44%.

In addition, he is being selective in the use of facts when he says 'The 2011 Scottish Parliament election showed that the Additional Member System is fit for purpose as it encourages participation and is more representative'. This is because according to source two the 2011 Scottish election had a turnout that was nearly 13% lower than the 2010 general election. This shows a huge difference in turnout. This is further emphasised by source two, which states that AMS is 'intended to reduce voter apathy and improve voter participation'.

However, David Watt is not being selective in the use of facts when he says 'The 2011 Scottish Parliament election showed that the Additional Member System is fit for purpose as it encourages participation and is more representative'. This is because according to source one AMS ensures greater proportionality, and this is backed up by source three, which shows that for the Lib Dems there was only a 1.4% difference between share of votes and share of seats, whereas under FPTP it was 12%.

Also, he is not being selective in the use of facts when he says that the 'Additional Member System … is more representative' as according to source two AMS is fairer to smaller parties as it has always returned representation, for example, in 2003 there were seventeen MSPs outside the main parties.

Marker's comments

This is an excellent answer as it shows integration of sources to explain selectivity in the use of facts. It also ensures that ALL sources are used and that examples BOTH of being selective and not being selective in the use of facts are used. Also, the candidate ensures that they quote from the sources and also uses the statistical evidence provided. Lastly, the candidate also attempts to evaluate the source by using phrases such as 'massive' and 'shows a huge difference'. **8 marks**

Hints & tips ★

Your answer must have some evidence of both being selective AND not being selective. Answers that look at only one side of selectivity can only gain a maximum of six marks.

Democracy in the United Kingdom

The following shows an example of how to use sources of information to identify and explain selective use of facts.

Skills question

Study sources one, two and three, below, then attempt the question that follows.

Source One

Male	49%
Female	51%
White	84%
Non-white background	16%

Gender and race in the United Kingdom

Party	Share of vote (%)
Conservatives	36.1
Liberal Democrats	23
Labour	29
Other	11.9
Coalition government	59.1
Opposition	37.9

2010 UK general election results

Source Two

Election ends in coalition

For the first time since 1974, the 2010 general election resulted in a coalition government being formed between the Conservatives and the Liberal Democrats. On 4th May, the Conservatives won the election with only a minority of the seats. After days of negotiations, a coalition agreement was reached between the Conservatives and the Liberal Democrats that resulted in a majority government. Many supporters of Labour felt aggrieved as their party gained many more seats than the Liberal Democrats, yet they are not part of the government.

First Past The Post is usually criticised for its poor representation for women, however the 2010 election returned the highest ever number of women MPs – 142. This constitutes 22% of the House of Commons. This has moved the UK from 79th in the world to joint 49th in the world for gender representation. There has also been an increase in the number of MPs from ethnic minority backgrounds from 14 in 2005 to 27 in 2010.

The UK government has embarked on the greatest shake-up of public services for three decades as they attempt to reduce the UK deficit. This has led to a record number of government defeats in the House of Commons. A controversial policy was the implementation of a £9,000 limit on the cost of university tuition in England and Wales. Following this there was a large scale riot in London. However, by 2013 the government was successful in partially reducing the UK deficit.

Source Three

Party	Number of seats	Seats %
Conservatives	307	47.3
Liberal Democrats	57	8.7
Labour	258	39.7
Other	28	4.3
Coalition	364	56
Opposition	286	44

2010 UK general election results

Using sources one, two and three, explain why the view of Tahir Mahmood is **selective in the use of facts**.

'The UK parliament is both effective in governing the country and representative of the people of the UK.'

Tahir Mahmood

In your answer you must:

- give evidence from the sources that supports Tahir Mahmood's view.
- give evidence from the sources that opposes Tahir Mahmood's view.

Your answer must be based on all three sources.

8 marks

Hints & tips

Your answer must have some evidence of both being selective AND not being selective. Answers that look at only one side of selectivity can gain a maximum of only six marks.

Chapter 14
Social Issues in the UK

Remember

A justifying a decision (options) question is worth ten marks — the highest mark available out of all the questions in the question paper, so it is important that you know how to pass it and use all the sources.

It is not the case that one option is correct and the other is incorrect; either can be chosen for full marks as evidence is contained within the sources to allow you to justify either decision or recommendation.

For full marks you must also explain why you have rejected the other option, if you do not do this the maximum mark you can achieve is eight.

Social inequality

The following shows an example of how to use sources of information to make and justify a decision.

Skills question

Study sources one, two and three, below, then attempt the question that follows.

You are a government adviser. You have been asked to recommend whether the government should introduce a tax on fizzy drinks ('fizz tax').

Option One	Option Two
Introduce a 'fizz tax'	Do not introduce a 'fizz tax'

Source One

According to a report by the Academy of Medical Royal Colleges, more than half of us will be overweight by 2050 and soft drinks are part of the problem. A quarter of British adults are already obese. The report suggested that fizzy drinks should be treated like cigarettes and stamped with a 20% tax. The cost to the NHS of treating obesity is increasing each year and is becoming unaffordable.

The report says that we are living in an environment where fizzy drinks that are bad for us are cheap and readily available, making the healthy choice the difficult choice for people who want help when it comes to being healthier. Most people think they should cut down on their consumption of fizzy drinks. The smoking ban was a success and now we need to take active steps to tackle the obesity problem.

Fizzy drinks have no nutritional value; they're just sugar and water. Even a small bottle of cola contains almost ten spoonfuls of sugar. The added sugar accelerates tooth decay, which affects nearly a third of adults and children. Despite not being listed as a risk factor by the National Osteoporosis Society, nutritional therapists believe the phosphoric acid preservative found in soft drinks can also affect calcium levels and contribute to poor bone density in young people.

How much disease and death do we have to experience before we accept that certain drinks are damaging to long-term health? With an existing tax in Norway linked to a significant decrease in the consumption of soft drinks, the Academy of Medical Royal Colleges believes that a 20% tax could garner similar results and help to tackle the obesity problem in Britain.

However, this is strongly disputed by those in the drinks industry.

Source: Adapted from the article *Can we fix obese Britain with a fizzy drinks tax?*, Metro, 28 February 2013

Source Two

Fizzy drinks are not listed as a risk factor by the National Osteoporosis Society. Soft drinks containing sugar contribute just 2% of the calories in the average diet. Over the past ten years, obesity rates have been going up but the consumption of soft drinks containing added sugar has actually gone down by 9%. Additionally, more than 60% of soft drinks contain no added sugar.

There is no single solution to the obesity problem and a sensible debate about all the factors involved is needed to help people make healthier choices. Most people will not change their habits and cut down on the amount of fizzy drinks they consume, anyway.

A 'fizz tax' could also have damaging effects on the manufacturing industry. It's worth noting that a similar tax in Denmark was scrapped at the end of last year because of concerns about its impact on jobs and competitiveness. And don't forget that soft drinks are already taxed. Soft drinks already carry VAT, so 10p from each 60p can of drink goes to the government. A further tax on a family's food and drink shopping bill would put yet more strain on people already hard-pressed during tough economic times. Health-related food taxes are regressive – that is, poor people pay a greater proportion of their income in tax than do the rich.

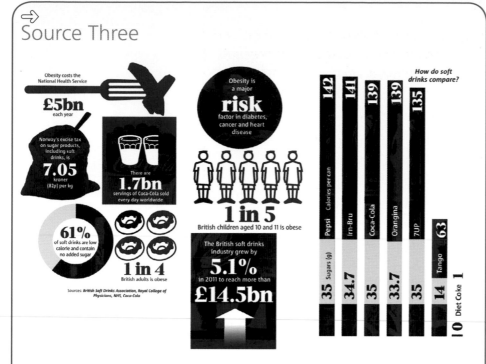

⇨ Source Three

Source: Metro

You must decide which option to recommend, **either** introduce a 'fizz tax' (Option 1) **or** do not introduce a 'fizz tax' (Option 2).

1 Using sources one, two and three, which option would you choose?
2 Give reasons to support your choice.
3 Explain why you did not choose the other option.

Your answer must be based on all three sources.   **10 marks**

Model answer

Option 1: Introduce a 'fizz tax'

The government should introduce a 'fizz tax' because we need to take active steps to tackle the obesity problem, which according to source one is one of the biggest public health threats of our time and is linked to drinking too much fizzy drink. This is backed up by source three, which shows that obesity is a major risk factor in diabetes, cancer and heart disease.

According to source one, the cost to the NHS of treating obesity is increasing each year and is becoming unaffordable. This is backed up in source three, which shows that obesity costs the NHS £5 billion each year. This tax will help to reduce some of these costs.

Source one says that an existing tax in Norway is linked to a significant decrease in the consumption of soft drinks and source three shows that obesity is a major risk factor in diabetes, cancer and heart disease. So reduced consumption leads to a decline in obesity and so a reduction in diabetes and heart disease. ⇨

According to source one, a quarter of British adults are already obese and more than half of us will be overweight by 2050, and soft drinks are part of the problem. This is backed up in source three, which shows that one in four adults and one in five children is obese. This tax will help to reduce these numbers of obese people.

I rejected Option 2 because despite source two saying that fizzy drinks are not listed as a risk factor by the National Osteoporosis Society, in source one nutritional therapists believe the phosphoric acid preservative found in soft drinks can affect calcium levels and contribute to poor bone density in young people.

Option 2: Do not introduce a 'fizz tax'

The government should not introduce a 'fizz tax' because according to source two more than 60% of soft drinks contain no added sugar, which is confirmed by source three, which shows that 61% of soft drinks contain no added sugar.

According to source two a 'fizz tax' could have damaging effects on the manufacturing industry. This is backed up in source three, which shows that the British soft drinks industry grew by 5.1% in 2011.

Source two says that soft drinks are already taxed with 10p from each 60p can of drink going to the government and source three shows that the soft drinks industry is worth £14.5 billion to the economy. A 'fizz tax' could lead to a cut in this revenue.

According to source two, soft drinks containing sugar contribute just 2% of the calories in the average diet, and according to source three 61% of soft drinks are low calorie, with Diet Coke having only one calorie per can.

I rejected Option 1 because despite source one saying an existing tax in Norway is linked to a significant decrease in the consumption of soft drinks, source two shows a similar tax in Denmark was scrapped at the end of last year because of concerns about its impact on jobs and competitiveness.

Marker's comment

Both answers are very well structured and make use of five paragraphs. The option chosen is clearly stated at the beginning of both answers.

Every paragraph in each of the two answers shows interaction between two sources. Evidence is accurate, detailed and relevant, with justification that is linked between two sources. Also, each answer has a reason why the other option was rejected, with accurate, detailed and relevant justification that is also linked between two sources.

So, overall two very good, high quality answers regardless of which option is chosen, and both deserving of full marks. **10 marks**

Crime and the law

The following shows an example of how to use sources of information to make and justify a decision.

Skills question

Study sources one, two and three below, then attempt the question that follows.

You are a Scottish government adviser. You have been asked to recommend whether or not to continue with the Community Payback Order for offenders.

Option One	Option Two
Continue with the Community Payback Order for offenders	Do not continue with the Community Payback Order for offenders

Source One

Selected facts and viewpoints

- Many prisons are full of offenders on short-term sentences who are of no threat to society and who are prevented from contributing to society.
- An offender on a Community Payback Order is seen by many as a prisoner escaping prison and undermines the public's idea of justice.
- When completing a Community Payback Order the personal help and advice given to offenders helps to reduce re-offending.
- For victims, knowing that the offender has not been sent to prison can cause stress and worry.
- It costs four times as much to send someone to prison for a short-term sentence, usually three months, than to have them carry out a Community Payback Order.
- Many offenders find a Community Payback Order harder than a prison sentence.
- Offenders already know the harm their actions cause – they do not need a Community Payback Order to tell them.
- Too many criminals are walking the street freely while completing their Community Payback Order.

Source Two

Results of opinion poll survey

Question 1: Were you aware of the harm your offending caused before your Community Payback Order started?

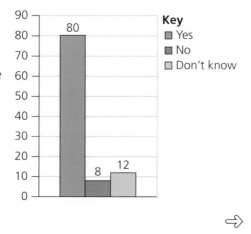

⇨

Question 2: Following completion of your Community Payback Order, how likely do you think it is that you will re-offend?

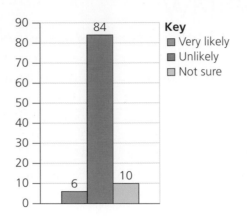

Source Three

View of Susan Harding	View of John Telford
The Community Payback Order sentence for offenders should continue. The law should not require that every offender is sent to prison. To reduce overcrowding in prisons, offenders who would normally receive a short-term prison sentence should serve their community as payback by doing something useful instead. Many offenders are unaware of the harm their offending causes to victims and society – Community Payback Orders help to change this. Community Payback Orders reduce the strain on prisoners' families. The size of the prison population and overcrowding need to be tackled, as well as reducing the huge cost of keeping people locked up, especially for short periods. Community Payback Orders are a cost-effective alternative to prisons and in many cases are more of a deterrent since offenders find them more demanding than prison.	The practice of Community Payback Orders should not continue. More and more criminals are carrying out serious crimes but are only being given Community Payback Order sentences as punishment. Prison is a deterrent; it protects the public from the individuals who are committing these crimes. The public is very unhappy with the current Community Payback Order system; especially when those completing Community Payback Orders go on to re-offend. The use of Community Payback Orders is an easy option for criminals and most don't even complete them. Community Payback Orders favour the prisoner not the victim since victims may suffer from stress and anxiety over a longer period of time. Stop Community Payback Orders and reassure the public that the offender is safely locked behind bars. Community Payback Orders simply keep offenders out of prison and free the group of offenders most likely to re-offend; they do not reduce re-offending rates.

You must decide which option to recommend, **either** continue with the Community Payback Order sentence for offenders (Option 1) **or** do not continue with the Community Payback Order sentence for offenders (Option 2).

1   Using sources one, two and three, above, which option would you choose?
2   Give reasons to support your choice.
3   Explain why you did not choose the other option.

Your answer must be based on all three sources.   **10 marks**

Model answer

Option 1: Continue with the Community Payback Order sentence

We should continue with the Community Payback Order sentence for offenders, because they help to reduce prison overcrowding. According to source one many prisons are full of offenders on short-term sentences who are of no threat to society and who are prevented from contributing to society. This is reinforced in source three, which states that to reduce overcrowding in prisons, offenders who would normally receive a short-term prison sentence should instead serve their community as payback by doing something useful.

Likewise, Community Payback Orders help to reduce re-offending. According to source one when completing a Community Payback Order the personal help and advice given to offenders helps to reduce re-offending. This is reinforced in source two, which shows that in an opinion poll survey most people are unlikely to re-offend after completing a Community Payback Order. In fact, 84% said they were very unlikely; this is a significant majority.

Also, Community Payback Orders are cheaper and would save money. This is highlighted in source one, which says that it costs four times as much to send someone to prison for a short-term sentence than to have them carry out a Community Payback Order. This is supported in source three, which states that Community Payback Orders are a cost-effective alternative to prisons and reduce the huge cost of keeping people locked up, especially for short periods.

Finally, as a punishment and deterrent, Community Payback Orders are not an easy or soft option. Source one says that many offenders find them harder than a prison sentence and this is confirmed in source three, which states that offenders find them more demanding than prison and in many cases this can make them more of a deterrent.

I rejected Option 2 because despite source three saying that Community Payback Orders simply keep offenders out of prison and free the group of offenders most likely to re-offend, I do not agree with this because in source two it shows that only 6% of those who complete them feel it is very likely they will re-offend. This is a very small minority compared to the 84% who feel it is unlikely.

Option 2: Do not continue with the Community Payback Order sentence

We should not continue with the Community Payback Order sentence for offenders, because many feel that they are a way of escaping justice. According to source one an offender on a Community Payback Order is seen by many as a prisoner escaping prison and this undermines the public's idea of justice. This is reinforced in source three, which states that the public is very unhappy with the current Community Payback Order system; especially when those completing Community Payback Orders go on to re-offend.

⇨

Likewise, they can favour the offender and not the victim. This is highlighted in source one, which states for victims knowing that the offender has not been sent to prison can cause stress and worry. This is reinforced in source three which says that Community Payback Orders favour the prisoner not the victim, since victims may suffer from stress and anxiety over a longer period of time.

Also, Community Payback Orders are not reliable or effective punishments for offenders. This is clearly shown in source one, which says that just 20% of Community Payback Orders were completed in Aberdeen in 2012. This is supported in source three, which states that their use is an easy option for criminals and most don't even complete them. Therefore, tougher sentencing is necessary.

Finally, Community Payback Orders make our streets unsafe. I know this because source one says that too many criminals are walking the street freely while completing their Community Payback Order. This is confirmed in source, which says that more and more criminals are carrying out serious crimes but are only being given Community Payback Order sentences to punish them. Surely, therefore, as source three says, prison protects the public from the individuals who are committing these crimes.

I rejected Option 1 because source three says that many offenders are unaware of the harm their offending causes to victims and society. This is untrue, because source two clearly shows that an opinion poll survey found that only 8% were unaware of the harm their offending caused, whereas a massive 84% were aware before their Community Payback Order started. This is a very large and significant difference.

Marker's comment

Both are very well structured answers making use of five paragraphs. The option chosen is clearly stated at the beginning of both answers.

Every paragraph in each of the two answers shows interaction between two sources. Evidence is accurate, detailed and relevant, with justification that is linked between two sources. Also, each has a reason why the other option was rejected with accurate, detailed and relevant justification that is also linked between two sources.

So, overall two very good, high quality answers regardless of which option is chosen, and both deserving of full marks. **10 marks**

Chapter 15
International Issues

World Powers

The following shows two examples of how to use sources of information to draw and support conclusions.

Remember

While your unit skills question may refer to the G20 country you have studied (or the European Union), the exam question may refer to real countries or may employ an 'enhanced reality' scenario.

Remember also that conclusion questions are worth eight marks and that for full marks you must use all the sources.

Skills question ?

Study sources one, two and three, below, and then answer the question that follows.

Source One

Education issues in a G20 African country

Since the end of discrimination progress has been made in improving education. Schools can no longer base their selection of pupils by race. Many black, coloured and Asian children now attend the former white state schools or private schools. In 2011 the government invested 21% of its entire budget on education. Compulsory education begins at age seven (Grade 1) and ends at age fifteen (Grade 9).

Free schooling has been introduced for the poorest 40% of students (all educated in black-only schools). The target is to increase this figure to 60%. This hopefully will encourage more black students to stay on at school. The Afrikaans Teachers' General Secretary stated that in 1997 1.6 million pupils started primary school, yet in 2009 only 370,000 completed their Matriculation exam.

Exam results have improved; in 1995 less than 50% of students passed and by 2011 this had increased to 70%. The number of students sitting the new National Senior Certificate (Matriculation exams) in 2010 was 570,000. However, inequalities remain between the poorer rural provinces like Eastern Cape and Mpumalanga and the urban richer provinces such as Western Cape and Gauteng. Again the racial differences in education still remain; most white children achieve high exam results and are educated in schools with excellent resources, while most black children achieve poor exam results and are educated in schools with limited resources. ⟹

Remember

It is good practice to use the bullet points as headings before using the sources or evidence to draw conclusions. Another good approach is to put your conclusion at the start or the end of the evidence. It is very important that you come to a conclusion about each statement, rather than simply writing out large pieces of sources without coming to a relevant conclusion.

Remember that when answering this question you must identify the correct conclusion for each of the three statements and provide evidence from across the sources.

Source Two

Province	Children aged 7–15 attending school (%)	Pass rate in the school leavers' exam (%)
Western Cape	98.5	82.0
Northern Cape	95.5	70.0
Free State	96.5	71.0
Gauteng	99.0	75.0
Kwazulu Natal	96.0	68.0
Limpopo	94.9	64.5
North West	96.0	69.0
Mpumalanga	92.0	55.0
Eastern Cape	93.4	56.7

Children attending school (%) and pass rate (%) by province

Source Three

Race	Pass rate (%)
Asian/Indian	90
Black	60
White	98
Coloured	80

School leavers' pass rate by race

	1995	2010
Male	16.2%	6.2%
Female	24.4%	9.8%

Persons aged over 25 with no formal education

Using sources one, two and three what **conclusions** can be drawn about education in this G20 African country?

You should reach a conclusion about each of the following:

- Racial differences in education.
- Provincial differences in wealth and education.
- Improvements in education over time.

Your conclusions must be supported by evidence from the sources. You should link information within and between sources in support of your conclusions.

Your answer must be based on all three sources.

When answering this question you must identify the correct conclusion for each of the three statements and provide evidence from across the sources.

8 marks

Model answer

Racial differences in education

The first conclusion is that racial differences in education still remain. Source one shows that schools with limited resources and with the poorest results are all black schools. This is also reflected in source three with the black students having the poorest exam results, with a pass rate of 60% compared to 98% for whites and Asians 90%.

Provincial differences in wealth and education

The conclusion is that the wealthiest provinces have the highest matriculation results and percentage of children attending school, and poorer provinces the lowest. Source one states that Western Cape and Gauteng are wealthy provinces and Mpumalanga and Eastern Cape are poor provinces. We can see in source two that the two wealthy provinces have the highest pass rates, for example the Western Cape 82%, and both have the highest percentage of children attending school. In contrast Mpumalanga and Eastern Cape have the lowest pass rates and percentage of children attending school, for example only 55% of Mpumalanga students passed the matriculation.

Improvements in education over time

The final conclusion is that education has improved since the end of apartheid. In source one it states that schools can no longer base their selection of pupils by race and many black, coloured and Asian children now attend the former white schools. Again, exam results have improved – in 1995 less than 50% passed and by 2011 it was 70%. This improvement is reflected in source three, which shows that the number of persons aged over 25 with no formal education has declined since 1995 for both males and females, for example for females it has declined from 24.4% to 9.8%.

Marker's comment

This is an excellent answer as the candidate uses separate paragraphs for each original statement. He makes an original conclusion in each paragraph and provides evidence from two sources to support each of his three conclusions. He provides detailed exemplification from the sources to further support his statement and he uses all three sources.

Each of the candidate's paragraphs are worth three marks each but as the maximum mark is eight, he is awarded eight.   **8 marks**

Remember

☞ You must make an original conclusion.

☞ You should use more than one source to support each original conclusion.

☞ Use all three sources in your answer.

☞ If you only use two sources the maximum mark you can achieve is six, and if only one source is used you can score only four marks.

Skills question

Study sources one, two and three, below, and then attempt the question that follows.

Source One

The death penalty in a G20 country

○ Black citizens make up 49% of those on death row but only 13% of the population.

○ While 65% of all murders involve black victims, 80% of death sentences involve white victims.

○ In Louisiana, the odds of a death sentence were 97% higher for those whose victim was white than for those whose victim was black.

○ A study in California found that those who killed whites were over three times as likely to be sentenced to death than those who killed blacks.

○ A study of the death penalty in North Carolina found that the odds of receiving a death sentence rose by 3.5 times among those murderers whose victims were white.

○ Almost 80% of death row defendants have been executed for killing white victims, even though in society as a whole black citizens account for about half of murder victims.

○ Race, along with geography, is an important factor in death penalty decisions. You are more likely to be executed in the south than anywhere else. Texas, in the south, has executed 493 people since 1976 compared to Connecticut, in the northeast, which has executed only one person.

Source Two

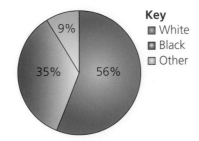

Race of murderers executed since 1976

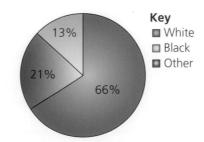

US population by race, 2012

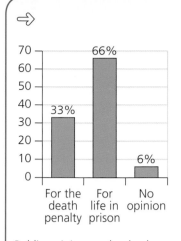

Public opinion on the death penalty

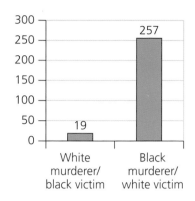

Persons executed for interracial murders

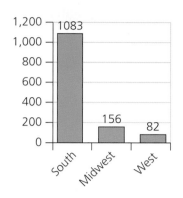

Executions in USA by selected region

Source Three

In 2010 an opinion poll found that:

- A clear majority of the public would choose a punishment of life in prison rather than the death penalty for murder.
- Police chiefs ranked the death penalty last among ways to reduce violent crime. The police chiefs also considered the death penalty to be the least efficient use of taxpayers' money.

Using sources one, two and three, above, what conclusions can be drawn about the death penalty in the USA?

You should reach a conclusion about each of the following:

- Race and the death penalty.
- Geography and the death penalty.
- Public opinion on the death penalty.

Your conclusions must be supported by evidence from the sources. You should link information within and between sources in support of your conclusions

Your answer must be based on all three sources.   **8 marks**

Model answer

Race and the death penalty

The conclusion is that there is discrimination by race and the death penalty in the USA. This conclusion is supported by evidence from source one, which says that in California those who killed whites were more than three times as likely to be sentenced to death as those who killed blacks. This is further supported in source two, which shows that since 1976 for interracial murders, 257 blacks have been executed for murdering whites while only nineteen whites have been executed for murdering blacks.

Geography and the death penalty

The conclusion is that the death penalty is not used equally in all states across the USA. This conclusion is supported by evidence from source one, which says that geography is an important factor in death penalty decisions and you are more likely to be executed in Southern states like Texas than Northeastern states like Connecticut. This is further supported in source two, which shows that the South has executed more people (1083) than any other region.

Public opinion on the death penalty

The final conclusion is that most people in the USA are against the use of the death penalty. This conclusion is supported by evidence from source three, which says that a clear majority of the public would choose a punishment of life in prison rather than the death penalty for murder and that police chiefs ranked the death penalty last among ways to reduce violent crime. This is further supported in source two, which shows that public opinion for the death penalty, at 33%, is well below that for life in prison, at 61%.

Marker's comment

This is an excellent answer as the candidate uses separate paragraphs for each original statement. She makes an original conclusion in each paragraph and provides evidence from two sources to support each of her three conclusions. The candidate provides detailed exemplification from the sources to further support her statement and uses all three sources.

Each of the candidate's paragraphs is worth three marks but as the maximum mark is eight, she is awarded eight. **8 marks**

World Issues

The following show examples of how to use sources of information to draw and support conclusions.

Remember

☞ You must make an original conclusion.

☞ You should use more than one source to support each original conclusion.

☞ Use all three sources in your answer.

☞ If you only use two sources the maximum mark you can achieve is six, and if you only use one source the maximum mark you can get is four.

Skills question

Study sources one, two and three, and then answer the question that follows.

Source One

Child soldiers around the world in 2013

There are still an alarming number of child soldiers in the world today. In our modern world no child should be subjected to the cruelties of war. For many, especially in Africa, this is still the case. In Africa there is an estimated 250,000 child soldiers in total. Many of these children live in countries locked in armed conflict. In Mali in 2013, Islamist terrorists recruited thousands of child soldiers to help take control of the country. Similarly, Sudan, Uganda and Somalia all have thousands of children who have been forced to participate in war. The DR Congo has the highest number of child soldiers on the continent.

Children are used as soldiers because they are easier to control and brainwash. They are treated horrifically as they may be starved of food, given drugs, abused, tortured or sent to fight on the front line of battle. Life for child soldiers is a life no child should experience. Furthermore, the psychological effects on children are felt long after they are finished fighting. Many child soldiers are desensitised to violence and have seen and done things that can leave lasting mental scars.

Children who have been affected by war require help to deal with trauma. The number of children who have been helped by charities in Africa has increased in recent years. Charities do good work in helping children overcome their experiences and move on to live as normal a life as they can.

Source Two

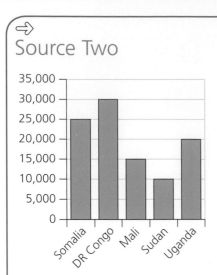

Estimated number of child soldiers in selected African countries

Source Three

Work done to help child soldiers

Many charities such as Combat Kids work very hard in helping child soldiers, especially if they have escaped or have been freed by their captors. Combat Kids reports that children have been forced to kill and fight. Combat Kids works to heal the scars left by war by providing counselling to children who have experienced war. They also rebuild schools destroyed by war and aim to get kids out of army uniforms and into school ones.

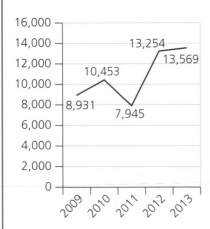

Children helped in Africa by Combat Kids in recent years

Using sources one, two and three, what **conclusions** can be drawn about child soldiers in the world?

You must reach a conclusion about **each** of the following:

- The number of child soldiers in selected African countries.
- The treatment of child soldiers by armed groups.
- Work done to help child soldiers.

Your conclusions must be supported by evidence from the sources. You should link information within and between sources in support of your conclusions.

Your answer must be based on all three sources.   **8 marks**

Model answer

The number of child soldiers in selected African countries

My first conclusion is that DR Congo has the highest amount of child soldiers whereas Sudan has the least. This is supported by evidence from source two that shows DR Congo has 30,000 child soldiers and Sudan has 10,000. Source one backs this up by stating 'The DR Congo has the highest count of child soldiers on the continent.'

The treatment of child soldiers by armed groups

The conclusion is that armed groups treat children badly. This conclusion is supported by evidence from source one, which states 'They are treated horrifically as they may be starved of food, given drugs, abused, tortured or sent to fight on the front line of battle'. This is backed up by source three, which states 'Combat Kids reports that children have been forced to kill and fight'.

Work done to help child soldiers

My conclusion is that charities are providing essential help to children affected by war. This conclusion is supported by evidence, firstly from source one, which states 'charities do good work in helping children overcome their experiences and move on to live as normal a life as they can'. This links in with source three, which states 'Combat Kids works to heal the scars left by war by providing counselling to children who have experienced war'. Also source three shows Combat Kids helped 13,569 child soldiers in 2013.

Marker's comment

This is an excellent answer and is well structured. The candidate makes an original conclusion at the beginning of each paragraph and uses two sources to back up each of the three conclusions. All three sources are used over the course of the answer. Clear linkage between sources has been made, which demonstrates a high level of aptitude in answering this type of enquiry skills question.

Each of the candidate's paragraphs is worth three marks but as the maximum mark is eight, he is awarded eight. **8 marks**

Remember

☞ You must make an original conclusion.
☞ You should use more than one source to support each original conclusion.
☞ Use all three sources in your answer.
☞ If you only use two sources the maximum mark you can achieve is six, and if only one source is used you can score only four marks.

Skills question

Study sources one, two and three, below, and then attempt the question that follows.

Source One

Terrorist activity around the world in 2012

The international community has had some success in recent years in the battle against terrorism. This has resulted in the number of terrorist-related incidents worldwide dropping from a high in 2008 to a low in 2012. The amount of incidents in individual countries has also come down, with the amount in Afghanistan decreasing. However, the number of terrorist incidents in Somalia and Spain has increased, which is a worrying trend. In Somalia much has to be done to return the rule of law to society as the country is suffering from political and economic failure.

The motives for terrorist incidents vary from country to country. In Afghanistan, Pakistan and Somalia the most common motive for terror was religious reasons. This is due to Islamic extremism in these countries. In Spain nationalist reasons was the main motive. The amount of deaths caused by terrorism remains very high even though the amount of terrorist incidents has dropped. More people died in terrorist incidents in Afghanistan than anywhere else, whereas the USA was the safest place from terrorism. In Pakistan a high number of deaths was caused by suicide attacks and car bombings.

Source Two

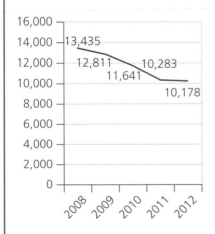

Number of terrorist incidents worldwide

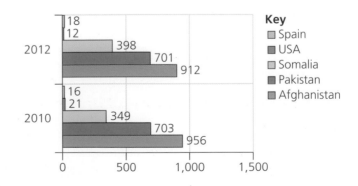

Key
- Spain
- USA
- Somalia
- Pakistan
- Afghanistan

Terrorist incidents in selected countries, 2010–2012

⇨
Source Three

	Motive for terrorist incidents, 2012			
Country	Religion	Nationalism	Political	Other
Afghanistan	546	179	156	31
Pakistan	478	102	98	23
Somalia	125	80	91	2
USA	4	1	5	2
Spain	4	11	2	1

Motive for terrorist incidents, 2012

Country	Deaths caused by terrorist incidents, 2012
Afghanistan	2,193
Pakistan	1,898
Somalia	1,012
USA	8
Spain	11

Deaths caused by terrorist incidents, 2012

Using sources one, two and three, what **conclusions** can be drawn about terrorism around the world?

You must reach a conclusion about **each** of the following:

- ○ Changes in the level of terrorist incidents worldwide.
- ○ Motives behind terrorist incidents in selected countries.
- ○ The level of terrorist incidents in selected countries.

Your conclusions must be supported by evidence from the sources. You should link information within and between sources in support of your conclusions.

Your answer must be based on all three sources. **8 marks**

Model answer

Changes in the level of terrorist incidents worldwide

My first conclusion is that the number of terrorist-related incidents has declined in recent years. Source one states 'the number of terrorist-related incidents worldwide dropping from a high in 2008 to a low in 2012'. This links with source two, which shows that in 2008 there were 13,435 incidents and in 2012 there were only 10,178, highlighting a significant decline.

Motives behind terrorist incidents in selected countries

My conclusion is that religion is the most common cause of terrorist incidents. This is supported by evidence from source three, which shows political reasons are the main cause of terrorism in the USA but that religion is the main cause in Afghanistan, Pakistan and Somalia with hundreds of incidents in these countries. This links in with source one, which states 'In Afghanistan, Pakistan and Somalia the most common motive for terror was religious reasons'.

The level of terrorist incidents in selected countries

My conclusion is that the level of terrorist incidents is decreasing in some countries but increasing in others. This is supported by evidence, firstly from source one, which states 'The amount of incidents in individual countries has also come down, with the amount in Afghanistan decreasing. However, the number of terrorist incidents in Somalia and Spain has increased, which is a worrying trend.' This links with source two, which shows that in 2010, Afghanistan suffered 956 terrorist incidents, then suffered fewer in 2012, with 912. Source two also shows the increase in Spain and Somalia – Spain increasing by two and Somalia by 49.

Marker's comment

This is an excellent answer and is well structured. The candidate makes an original conclusion at the beginning of each paragraph and uses two sources to back up each of the three conclusions. All three sources are used over the course of the answer. Clear linkage between sources has been made, which demonstrates a high level of aptitude in answering this type of enquiry skills question.

Each of the candidate's paragraphs is worth three marks but as the maximum mark is eight, he is awarded eight.　　　　　　**8 marks**